BASICS of Windows®

BASICS of Windows®
The Easy Guide to Your PC

Stephie Smith

Copyright

Dedication

One day I had a wonderful idea. Wouldn't it be great if I set my mother up with a computer so she could email her sisters? The more I thought about it, the more excited I became, and I just knew Mom would be forever grateful. Of course, she'd never actually seen a computer, let alone used one, but I would quickly teach her what she needed to know.

I made everything easy for her. I put a shortcut to the email program on her Windows® Desktop, and I set things up so that with a click of a button, she could dial up on the modem and connect to her email. I wrote down these simple instructions:

1) Click once on Desktop Shortcut.
2) Press Enter.

I was so proud. (I had no idea what I was getting into.)

Two days later Mom called in tears to say she'd searched her entire desk and the shortcut was nowhere to be found. Her biggest fear was that it had gotten stuck to the cat and he'd eaten it, or else it had fallen off somewhere in the house.

"Huh?" I said.

It took me a minute to realize she'd been searching for the email shortcut on the top of her office desk—the desk her cat likes to nap on—instead of looking on her *Windows* Desktop. And she obviously didn't remember what a "shortcut" was either.

And *that* was only the beginning.

So, this book is dedicated to my mother, Ruth Welch Smith, for her inspiration ... however unintentional.

Contents

Introduction

In 1988 my boss purchased a computer to track inventory. When no one was looking, I touched it. The screen went dark except for the words "Security violation. This computer is now locked." It took three days for the inventory specialist to get back into the computer and, in the meantime, co-workers gave me accusing looks. I didn't touch another computer for two years.

In 1990 I took a word processing course and I gained so much confidence I was eager to show off to a friend. Within minutes I had locked up his PC. When he rebooted, a message said, "Internal failure. Insert boot-up disk to reformat drive." He didn't have a boot-up disk and we wouldn't have known what to do with it if he had. He was forced to hire a *real* computer expert and I resolved to keep my hands off everyone else's PCs.

But I was determined to conquer this new technology. It obviously wasn't going away, and it didn't seem realistic to think I could get rid of it one PC at a time.

I worked hard at my studies and I became proud of my increasing knowledge. So proud, in fact, that I must have bragged (although it certainly isn't like me) to my sister because she called to say she'd given my number to an 83-year-old man who had just purchased a Windows 95 PC. *Gulp.*

I hadn't seen Windows 95 so I borrowed a set of videos on the subject and took notes. The man was a quick learner and was able to perform all the tasks I gave him during the first lesson. Unfortunately, when I returned several days later, he couldn't remember how to do any of those things, and neither could I. Mumbling something about how important it was that he figure it out on his own, I slinked from the house (I'm not proud of this). But I returned the next day with exercises and handout pages that he could keep for review.

I was relieved when his tutoring was over. Then the phone calls began. He had told a friend who told a friend who told a friend. I couldn't say no. I didn't have a job and my cats liked to eat—a lot.

So that's how this book began: as handout pages for people who wanted to learn the basics of using their Windows computer, quickly and without reading a 400-page book.

Why this book isn't version-specific

Certain things are basic to every Windows operating system, and if you learn the basics and refuse to be intimidated, you can get on any PC and figure out the rest. And that's my goal: to enable you to get on a PC at your next job interview or at the library or at school, with the confidence that you'll be able to do what you need to do. That's where the exercises are especially helpful. Though simple, they force you to try things by giving you specific tasks to perform.

Finally, because weird things *will* happen, I've added a Questions & Answers chapter, hoping to cover many of the annoying things that might pop up, sometimes literally.

So … I hope you'll use this book as it was written to be used: to learn the basic skills and to gain enough confidence to realize that from there, you can go anywhere!

Instructions for using this Book

Here are some facts that will help you make the most of this book:

Numbering System

When items are **numbered with a period**, they are steps to follow in order. Example:

1. Do this first.
2. Do this second.
3. Do this third.

When items are **numbered with parentheses and the word "OR" is used to separate them**, they are different ways to perform the same task. Example:

(1) You can do this, OR
(2) You can do this, OR
(3) You can do this.

When items are **numbered with square brackets**, the numbered items correspond to numbered items in a picture. Example:

[1] Definition/description of picture item 1.
[2] Definition/description of picture item 2.
[3] Definition/description of picture item 3.

Bulleted Lists

Bulleted items are separate pieces of information about a topic. Example:

* The Minimize button displays a hyphen.
* The Maximize button is a square.
* The Restore button is a double square.

Quotation Marks

* When a book section is referred to, it will be in quote marks. Example: See "Mouse Properties" in Chapter 3.

- When Windows text in a window, folder, pop-up, etc., is referred to directly in an explanation or description, it will be in quote marks. Ex: If you mouse over the item, a "What's This?" may pop up.

Italics

Windows options you are to click on, mouse over, or select will be italicized. Ex: Click *OK* to exit the menu.

Capitalization

Windows items such as Desktop, Taskbar, Title Bar, etc., will only be capitalized the first few times they are used unless referred to as a title.

Navigating and File/Folder Paths

Where I display ">" between programs, folders, or files, it means *Go here first > Then proceed here > Then here*—a navigation path, which is very similar to a file path. So, for example, *Start button > All Programs > Accessories > Calculator* would mean that you click on the *Start* button, then on *All Programs*, then on *Accessories*, then on *Calculator.*

A file path can be represented this way, and it may also be represented with back slashes. More about that in Chapter 11.

Version Specifics

Information in this book applies to Windows XP, Windows Vista, and Windows 7. Whenever information applies to one version and not the others, I will state that fact (e.g., *Windows 7 only*) so that you'll know it doesn't apply to all three versions. In the screen shot captions, I usually note which version was used for the picture, but that's just for your information. Again, if I show a picture of something that doesn't exist in all three versions, I will state so specifically.

1 - What is Windows?

Windows® is a software program that controls your computer and everything on it. A software program that does this is called an operating system (OS) software. Some other operating systems are Microsoft DOS® (Disk Operating System) and Mac OS® (Macintosh Operating System, used on Apple® computers).

Fig. 1-1. Windows software cover (XP Home Edition).

Operating system softwares are one type of software. There are software programs for anything and everything: typing letters, editing photos, creating spreadsheets, developing databases, playing games, creating websites. If you can think of it, there's probably a software for it, and some of them do more than one thing. But none of these other software applications will work without an operating system.

This book is about the Windows® operating system, which controls everything on (or hooked up to) your PC. But Windows isn't just an operating system, because along with it—depending on the version

you have—you get games, text editing applications, and other software programs that are included as part of the package.

The next page will give you a brief overview of your Windows
Desktop, and then you'll learn about using your mouse.

2 - What Is The Windows Desktop?

The Windows Desktop is what shows up on your monitor screen when you start your computer—after the login screen, if you have one, but before you open anything else. It's the background on which everything happens.

It has a color, pattern, or picture, which you can change. It will have at least one icon (a small graphic that represents an application, folder, or file). That icon may be the *Recycle Bin*. Your version of Windows may also have an icon called *My Computer* or *Computer* and/or *My Documents/Documents*. If not, you can add those and others.

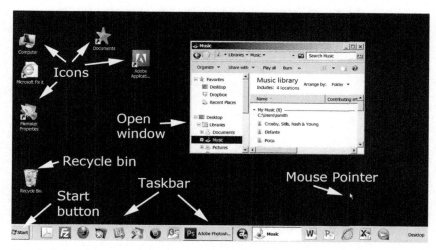

Fig. 2-1. Desktop showing icons, Taskbar, Start button, mouse pointer, and an open folder (Windows 7, modified Classic Theme).

On the Desktop will be the Taskbar on which you'll see a Start button. The button says *Start* in XP; beginning with Vista, that word was removed unless you're using a Classic desktop theme, and the terminology was changed from "Start button" to "Windows Orb." I use both terms in this book. Every application, folder, or file will open into a window on this Desktop.

The pointer for your mouse should also show on the Desktop.

3 - Using A Mouse

If you're a beginner, move your mouse around on the mouse pad. You'll see your mouse pointer move on your Windows desktop. **To select an item**, move your mouse so that the pointer is over that item and then click. The mouse also comes in handy for discovering information about an item. Move the mouse slowly over the item (called **mouse over**) to see if any explanations pop up.

Don't be afraid of your mouse. If you accidentally click on something, or change your mind, just click on an empty area of the Desktop or Taskbar or an empty area of an open window, or press the Esc (Escape) button on your keyboard.

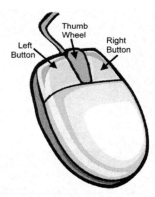

Fig. 3-1. A typical mouse with left button, thumbwheel, and right button.

The following instructions are for right-handers, which is the default mouse set-up in Windows. To switch (if you're left-handed), see "Changing Your Mouse Settings" later in this chapter.

If you have a laptop and use a touchpad instead of a mouse, read these mouse instructions for general information, and then see the specific instructions for a touchpad.

Left Button

The left button is for selecting and opening items. It's also used to select text and to move items (called drag and drop). You single-click to select and double-click to open with the left button.

Right Button

The right button allows you to not only select an item, but also to apply an action to it. When you right-click on an item, a menu opens. The menu choices will change, depending on the item and your version of Windows. There's no double-clicking with the right button.

Usually when instructions say to click without specifying right or left, it's a left-click because the left button was considered the primary button (in the beginning, it was the *only* button). But try right-clicking first.

Thumbwheel

Your mouse may have a thumbwheel between the buttons. **A thumb-wheel has multiple uses:**

- **Scrolling.** Click in the window and then move the thumbwheel up or down to move items in a window past your view, or to move between pages displayed vertically in a document, or to move from one record to the next in a database. Some mice can scroll horizontally as well as vertically. (Note: If you don't have a thumb-wheel, you can scroll in a window using the keyboard too. Just click in the window and press the Up, Down, Left, and Right arrow keys.) See "Scrolling to See A Window's Content" in Chapter 7 for more.

  You can **lock the thumbwheel in Scroll mode** by pressing down on it. Then just move your mouse up (forward on the mouse pad) or down without touching the wheel. When you've finished scrolling, press the thumbwheel again to unlock it.

- **Increase or decrease the display size of items.** Click inside a window, hold down the Ctrl key (usually located in the lower left and/or right corner of your keyboard) and move the thumbwheel up. The display size of the window will increase. This is also good for reading small text on websites or in documents. If you prefer to zoom out to see the entire page, hold down the Ctrl key and move the thumbwheel down. (Note: If you don't have a thumbwheel, you can zoom in and out by holding down the Ctrl key and pressing the plus sign to zoom in and the minus sign to zoom out.)

Single Click with the Left Button

A single click with the left button only *selects* the item your pointer is over—so you can do something else with that item, such as open it, make a copy of it, delete it, or move it to another location.

A selected item of any type (icon, file, folder, window) will look different from the other items. It may change color, it may be highlighted (brighter or darker), or it may have a border around it. Note that the words *highlighted* and *selected* and *active* are used interchangeably. When something is highlighted, it's emphasized in some way, and it will be the active/selected item.

Fig. 3-2. *Computer* is the selected icon on the desktop.

If an icon has a curved arrow pointing at it, as with *My Documents* in Fig. 3-2, it's a **shortcut** to a file or folder, not the *actual* file or folder. For more on shortcuts see "Creating Shortcuts to Programs, Folders, or Files" in Chapter 11.

In Fig. 3-3, the first item (My Music) is selected. Note how both the folder name and the icon that represents the folder are highlighted.

Fig. 3-3. Folder in Details view with *My Music* as the selected item.

When selecting an icon, you may accidentally select just the name and your mouse pointer may turn into a blinking text cursor. If this happens, click on an empty area of your desktop to deselect, then click again on the icon *picture*, not the name. (Renaming folders and files is covered in Chapter 11.)

Single Click with the Right Button

A single click with the right button brings up a menu that offers choices, depending on what type of item (icon, file, folder, window) you clicked. See Fig. 3-4 where I right-clicked on a folder called *My Web Sites* inside *My Documents*.

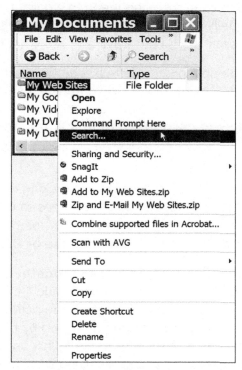

Fig. 3-4. The right-click menu for *My Web Sites* folder gives me options to apply to that folder (Windows XP).

The right-click menu for *My Web Sites* lists the most common tasks that can be performed on a *folder*, since that's what I right-clicked on. Note in Fig. 3-4 that some choices on the menu (such as *Send To*) show **a triangle pointing to the right** and some (such as *Search,* selected in Fig. 3-4 above) show an **ellipsis.** In both cases this means more items are available. If you click on an item with an ellipsis, a ***separate*** window or menu usually pops opens. If you mouse over or click an item with a triangle, an **attached** cascading menu usually appears. Sometimes a cascading window has several tiers.

With the menu in Fig. 3-4, I can copy the entire folder, delete the folder, rename the folder, search the folder, etc. If you have the same version of Windows that I had in this picture, you still may not have the same choices available to you; i.e., if you don't have SnagIt or AVG softwares as my PC did, those choices won't be on your menu.

Move the mouse pointer down the menu to highlight your choice and click. You can usually either right or left-click, but on some PCs you may have to left-click. Try it both ways and see what happens.

If you choose to do nothing, just left-click on an empty area of the desktop, an empty area of a folder, an empty place on the taskbar, or on the title bar of any open folder, or press your Esc key. **You can press the ESC key to escape out of just about anything.**

Selecting Multiple Items

As mentioned, you can select one item by clicking on it with your mouse. To select more than one item—perhaps to delete several files or move them to another folder—use your keyboard's **Ctrl button or Shift button in conjunction with the mouse or the arrow keys:**

- **To select individual items that aren't together, hold down the Ctrl key** and click on each item. Release the Ctrl key when you've selected the items you want, then apply the action to all selected files at one time. If you're applying an action by right-clicking, select the items as described, then right-click on *one* of them. See Fig. 3-5 where I selected two items using the Ctrl key.

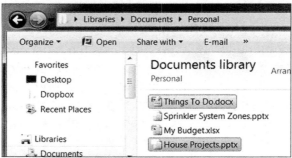

Fig. 3-5. Selecting non-adjacent items using the Ctrl key (Windows 7).

- **To select items that are together, select the first item, then hold down your Shift key and select the last item.** All items between the first and last will be selected. This works whether you are viewing folder items as a list or as icons/thumbnails. If you're selecting icons, however, Windows will select icons across the window and then down, while items in a list are selected down and then across.

In Fig. 3-6 I clicked on the same two items that I clicked on in Fig. 3-5, only this time I pressed the Shift key (instead of the Ctrl key) before selecting the second item. Those two files and the two files between them were selected.

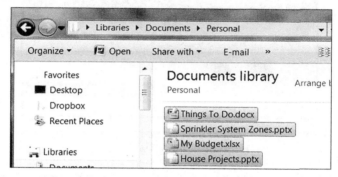

Fig. 3-6. Selecting adjacent items using the Shift key (Windows 7).

See "Drag and Drop" later in this chapter for another way to select multiple items at once.

Double Click (left button only)

A double left-click (with clicks close together) selects and opens the item. Here are some other ways to open an item:

(1) Left-click the item to select it, then press the Enter key, OR
(2) Right-click on the item and when a menu opens, move your mouse pointer up or down the menu to highlight the word *Open* and click, OR
(3) Change the way your mouse works so that a single click opens an item. See below.

Setting Mouse to Open Items with a Single Click

To change your mouse so that a single click, rather than a double click, opens items, follow the steps below. First you'll need to get to your Folder Options menu in order to make the change.

1. Open *My Computer* or any folder following the previous instructions.
2. Once the folder is open, click on *Tools* as in Fig. 3-7.
3. Move your mouse down the drop-down menu and click on *Folder Options.* The menu in Fig. 3-9 will open.
4. Once you're in the Folder Options menu (see Fig. 3-9), click in the circle that says "Single-click to open an item" and click OK. If you don't like the result, change your setting back.

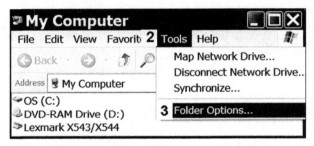

Fig. 3-7. Navigating to the *Folder Options* menu in XP, Vista, or Windows 7. The menu in Fig. 3-9 will then open.

Fig. 3-8 shows a second way to get to the Folder Options menu if you have Windows 7.

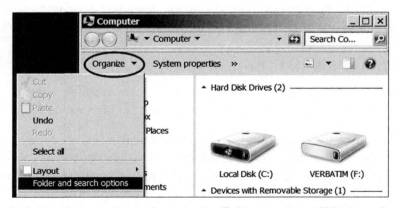

Fig. 3-8. Another way to navigate to the Folders options, Windows 7 only. Click on *Organize*, then *Folder and search options.* The menu in Fig. 3-9 will then open.

Whether you take the route of Fig. 3-7 or Fig. 3-8, the menu in Fig. 3-9 is the result.

Fig. 3-9. Folder Options menu: changing mouse-click
default from double-click to single-click.

Note: The Folder Options menu doesn't have any other mouse
options. To make other changes to your mouse operation, follow the
instructions in the section "Changing Your Mouse Settings" at the end
of this chapter.

Drag and Drop

Drag and drop is the easiest way to move or copy a file or folder
with your mouse—as long as both **the location you're copying**
from and the **location you're copying** *to* are visible from your
desktop. When both locations are visible:

• To **move** the item, left-click to select it, but instead of releasing the
button, continue to hold the button down while you drag the item
to the new location. Then release your mouse button.

• To put a **copy** of the item in another location (so it will be in both
places), hold down your Ctrl key before you left-click. You'll see a
little plus mark (+) beside the pointer as you drag the item to the
new location. Then release your mouse button.

You can drag and drop with the right button too. Right-click
and drag the item to its new location. When you release the mouse

button, a menu will open and you can choose *Move* or *Copy*. (When using the right button to copy an item, don't hold down the Ctrl key.)

To cancel in the middle of a drag and drop: if using the left button, press the *Esc* key while still holding the button down; if using the right button, release the button and select *Cancel*.

If the location you're copying to isn't visible on your desktop, right-click on the item and select *Copy* with the left button. Then go to the new location, right-click and select *Paste*.

Dragging with the mouse can also be used **to select multiple items.** In Fig. 3-10, I clicked with the mouse where the X is (upper left corner), held down the mouse button and dragged diagonally (see arrow), and released the mouse button where the circle is around the mouse pointer. By dragging this way I selected two picture files, as shown by the selection rectangle around them. If I had changed the angle of my drag so that I was dragging further to the right, I could have included the two pictures in the middle column.

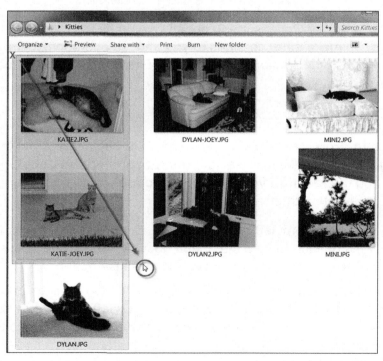

Fig. 3-10. Dragging to select multiple items in a window (Windows 7).

To select these two pictures without dragging, I'd click on the top left picture, hold down my Ctrl button, and click on the second picture to add it to my selection. Holding down the *Shift* key instead of the *Ctrl* key, would have included the other two pictures in the top row as well, since the shift key selects the first and last and all in between, and Windows selects thumbnails across and then down.

Changing your Mouse Settings

There are several mouse settings you can change. These include switching the primary and secondary buttons (for right-handed versus left-handed usage), the double-click speed, the mouse pointer size and action, and thumbwheel operation. Most of these settings are in the Mouse folder in the Control Panel, and there's more than one way to get to your Mouse folder.

(1)   In Windows 7, right-click on your desktop and click on *Person-alize*. Then click on *Change mouse pointers.* The Mouse Proper-ties menu will open, OR

(2)   In any version, click on your *Start* button and then click on *Control Panel.* If your Control Panel is set to Category View as in Fig. 3-11, click on the category called *Printers and Other Hard-ware* (XP and Vista), or *Hardware and Sound* (Windows 7). Then click on the Mouse icon or the word Mouse (it may be under another sub-category called *Devices and Printers*).

Your Control Panel may be set to one of several views. In XP/Vista your choices are Category View or Classic View. In Windows 7 your choices are Category, Small Icons, or Large Icons. Category View groups items together, though, interestingly, the same items are not grouped together across different versions of Windows. The other views—Classic, small icons, large icons—display the items individu-ally, not grouped into categories. How to tell what view you're in:

• In XP or Vista, you can tell by the choice you're given for changing the view. In Fig. 3-11, in the upper left of the window, it says "Switch to Classic View" which shows you're in Category View.

• In Windows 7, in the upper right of your window, you'll see a "View by:" and that will show you (see Fig. 3-12 below). Click on the triangle to the right of the listed view and try the others out.

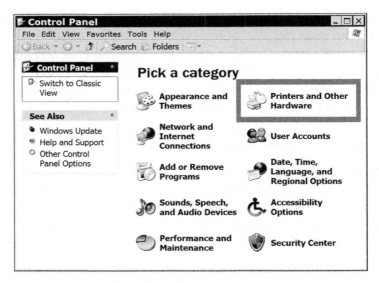

Fig. 3-11. Control Panel: navigating to the Mouse folder in XP.

Windows shows icons alphabetically *across* the window, rather than *down* (see Fig. 3-12). To force the icons into a vertical alphabetical list, resize the window narrower so that only one column shows. See Chapter 7 to learn how to resize your windows.

Fig. 3-12. Control Panel in Small Icons view in Windows 7, Classic theme.

Mouse Properties

In the Mouse Properties menu (Fig. 3-13), click on each tab across the top. Notice how a tab changes when you select it. The title will stay in the same place, but the tab will move to the front. There may be other differences that tell you a tab is selected. In different versions of Windows, the tabs may show different options.

Buttons tab

In Fig. 3-13, the Buttons tab is the selected tab. The selected tab is a brighter shade of white and there is a thicker line above the title.

Fig. 3-13. Selected "Buttons" tab in the Mouse Properties menu (XP).

The Buttons tab usually allows left-handed people to switch the mouse buttons so that the right button is the primary button (you can also get to this setting from any folder as mentioned previously in "Setting Mouse to Open Items with a Single Click"). Or you can set your mouse with "click lock," which allows you to click once with your primary button to set the button in the "click" mode so you can drag items without holding the button down. You can also change your double-click speed (i.e., how fast you must click two clicks together in order for Windows to realize you are double-clicking), and you can test out the speed by double-clicking on the folder shown in the rectangle below.

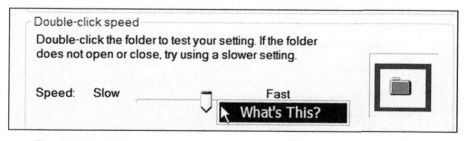

Fig. 3-14 Double-click speed adjustment on the Buttons tab (Vista).

Sometimes if you right-click on an adjustment or option, a "What's This?" will pop up as in Fig. 3-14. Click on *What's This?* and an explanation will appear.

Pointers tab

You can change the way your mouse pointer looks by choosing
a different scheme on the Pointers tab. Click on the drop-down menu
(see Fig. 3-15, inside the drawn rectangle) and you'll see a list of
various schemes to choose from.

In Fig. 3-15 I chose the scheme called "Magnified." It's the same as
the regular scheme but the pointers are larger. The various pointers
that go with each action in the scheme are displayed in the white
area of the menu. Click on one of the pointer choices and the pointer
will be displayed in the area where the circle is. You can choose an
overall theme, but change individual pointers within that scheme as
well. If you do make any changes, you'll be asked to give the pointer
theme a new name.

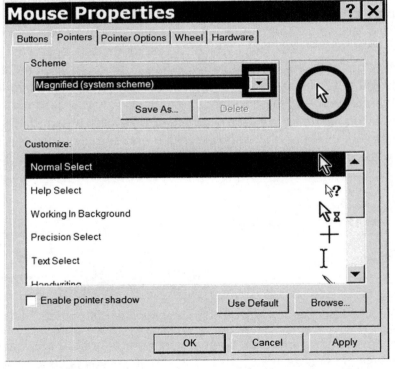

Fig. 3-15. Choosing a different mouse scheme in the Mouse Properties
menu, Pointers tab (XP theme).

The Mouse Properties menu, like all properties menus in Windows,
has three selections for applying changes and closing the menu:

- **Click *Cancel* to exit and no changes will be made**. This is good if you just want to look at your options and then close the menu.

- **Click *OK* to accept *all* changes**. This is good if you've made changes and want to accept them and exit the Mouse menu.

- **Click *Apply* to apply the current action to the item** you want to change without closing the menu. This is good if you want to go through tab by tab, making choices and applying them as you go. After you're finished applying changes, click *OK* to exit the menu.

Pointer Options tab

- **Select a pointer speed** (slider bar): Dragging the sliding bar closer to *Fast* means that the pointer will move farther across the screen with less movement of the mouse.

- **Enhance pointer precision** (checkbox): This makes the mouse go slower as it approaches objects, which means you have to move your mouse more.

- **Snap to** (checkbox): Moves the mouse pointer automatically to the default choice and then all you have to do is press your Enter key to accept the choice. For example, if a menu has the choices of *OK* and *Cancel*, *OK* is probably the default choice, which you'll be able to tell because it will be highlighted in some way.

- **Visibility choices** (checkbox): This will help you find or hide your pointer. If you search for your mouse pointer a lot, click in the checkbox that says "Show location of pointer when I press the Ctrl key." Then press the Ctrl key when you lose your mouse pointer. When you release the key, a large circle will zoom in to your pointer.

Wheel tab

The wheel tab options are for the mouse thumbwheel. If scrolling with your wheel makes the web page scroll too fast, you can slow it down by reducing the number of lines that one notch scrolls, if that option is available, or by moving the slider bar closer to *Slow*.

Hardware tab

Hopefully, you won't need to do anything with the Hardware tab. If you hook up a new mouse, do so before you start your PC, and Windows should notice it and find the correct mouse driver (the software that controls the hardware) or tell you to insert the CD that came with the device. If you have an Internet connection, Windows may find and install the software for you.

Other types of Mice

I've described the typical mouse. You may prefer to use a roller ball, a touch/trackpad, or a pen stylus (great for drawing) instead. All devices have buttons to click. The difference is mostly in what you move around: a mouse or a pen on a pad (though some pens are moved on the monitor screen), a ball that's seated and rolls around in a base, a rubber button the size of a pencil eraser, or your finger on a tracking surface. What you get used to is probably what you'll keep using, so if you're not sure what's best for you, go to your local computer store and try them all out.

If you'll be using a laptop most of the time, consider learning the touchpad because a mouse or a stylus pen will need to be connected as a separate piece of hardware, and that takes some of the convenience away from the laptop.

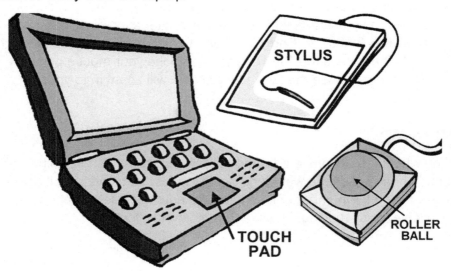

Fig. 3-16. Laptop Touchpad, Pen Stylus, Roller Ball.

Touchpad/Trackpad Tips

To use the touchpad instead of the mouse (note: different manufacturers may have different options):

- **move the on-screen pointer:** Drag your finger on the pad.
- **left-click:** Tap one finger OR press the left touchpad button.
- **right-click:** Tap two fingers OR press the right touchpad button.
- **drag and drop:** Tap, then tap again and slide your finger, OR
  hold the left touchpad button down and slide your finger.
- **scroll:** Slide two fingers horizontally or vertically, OR slide one
  finger vertically along the right edge of the pad and one finger
  horizontally along the bottom edge of the pad.

The touchpad software comes from your laptop's manufacturer, not
from Windows, but it is included in the operating system. To look at or
change your touchpad settings, try these things:

(1) Check the Mouse Properties menu for a Touchpad/Trackpad tab,
     OR
(2) Check your Devices and Hardware folder (located at *Start >
     Control Panel* OR *Start > Devices and Hardware*) and look for
     Touchpad/Trackpad, OR
(3) Look in the Notification Area/System Tray on the Taskbar for a
     touchpad icon, OR
(4) Search on the Internet for your manufacturer, version of
     Windows, and touchpad settings, e.g., "HP laptop touchpad
     settings windows 7" and read through the search results, OR
(5) Go to your manufacturer's website and search for "touchpad
     driver." It's possible you have an old driver and can download a
     newer driver from their website. If your driver is the latest and
     you're not happy with it, consider installing a third party driver.
     Your manufacturer may offer information on that.

Using Keyboard Shortcuts instead of your Mouse

Here are some keyboard shortcuts that can be substituted for mouse
actions. When I use the + sign below, it means "and," so, for instance,
Ctrl+C means hold down the Ctrl key *and* press the letter C.

Shortcuts using the Ctrl key

Ctrl+C = Copy
Ctrl+V = Paste
Ctrl+X = Cut
Ctrl+A = Select All

For **Copy** and **Cut**, select the item first. If you select the item and
Copy, then go to another folder and *Paste*, you'll paste a copy. If you
Cut instead of *Copy*, you'll move that item, not copy it to a second
location. To move all items in a folder or all the text in a document,
click anywhere inside the folder window (or document) and press
Ctrl+A to **Select All**.

Ctrl+Z = Undo (an action)
Ctrl+Y = Redo (an action)

Undo and **Redo** can be used in most places, but don't select the
item first. Windows assumes you are undoing or redoing your last
action. You can put an item in the Recycle Bin and then *Undo* to
restore the item to its original location. You can delete a paragraph in
Microsoft Word and then *Undo* to restore it and then *Redo* to delete it
again.

Ctrl+F = Find

Use **Find** in a program or folder when you're looking for something.
If you're in Internet Explorer and press Ctrl+F, the Find box will open
at the top of the page so you can type a word or phrase for searching
that web page.

Ctrl+B = Bold
Ctrl+I = Italics
Ctrl+U = Underline

Bold, **Italics**, and **Underline** have shortcuts in Microsoft programs
such as Microsoft Word, Microsoft PowerPoint, etc. You can either
select the text and press Ctrl+B to apply a bold style to the selection,
or you can press Ctrl+B, which will turn on the Bold styling, type the
words (they will appear in Bold), then press Ctrl+ B again to turn off
the Bold styling. Same goes for Ctrl+I for italics and Ctrl+U for under-
lining.

Ctrl+N = New Document
Ctrl+S = Save Document
Ctrl+P = Print Document
Ctrl+W = Close Window
Ctrl+Q = Quit Program

The above shortcuts work in most programs, not just Microsoft programs. For example, while I'm typing this document in Adobe's InDesign, if I press Ctrl+N, the InDesign "New Document" dialog box will open. If I were in Microsoft Word, a new Microsoft Word document menu would open.

Every program you use will have shortcut keys. If you click on the menu items, such as *File, Edit, Layout,* etc., across the top of that program's window, you'll see the shortcuts noted next to the items on the drop-down menus.

Shortcuts using the Function keys

The Function keys (F1 through F12) located across the top of your keyboard offer easy ways to perform some tasks. Pressing just the function key will give one result, and that result will be different depending on what software program you're in or what you're doing at the time you press the key. Pressing Ctrl, Shift, or Alt plus the function key will give you another result.

F1 = access Help for whatever program you are in
F2 = rename the selected item
F3 = search for a file or folder
F4 = display the address bar list in Internet or Windows Explorer
F5 = refresh the active window in Internet or Windows Explorer
F11 = full screen mode in web browser; press F11 again to return to normal screen mode

To see what the function keys do in a particular program, click on Help(?) in that program and search for "Function keys." Or press the keys, trying the combinations with Ctrl, Shift, and Alt. You can press the Esc key to escape from any action you begin.

Shortcuts using the Windows logo key

Windows logo key = open or close the Start menu (this is one that's really convenient)
Windows logo key+D = display the desktop
Windows logo key+E = open *Computer*
Windows logo key+F = search for a file or folder
Windows logo key+L = lock your computer or switch users
Windows logo key+T = cycle through programs on the taskbar
Windows logo key+Tab = cycle through programs on the taskbar using Aero Flip 3-D (Windows Flip)
Windows logo key+spacebar = preview the desktop

There are many more shortcuts. To see a complete list for your version of Windows, search the Internet for "keyboard shortcuts available in Windows XP" and substitute XP for your version of Windows. Look through the search results for links that have "microsoft.com" in them and click on those. Microsoft has the most complete lists.

4 - Versions of Windows®

New Version or Upgrade?

Each new release of Windows is not necessarily an upgrade or a later version of the previous version sold because they don't all use the same technology. Some versions were designed for the consumer market for personal and home computing, while others were designed for the enterprise market. Purchasing an upgrade is usually cheaper than purchasing a new version of Windows, but it's not always better. Your PC may not be able to run the upgraded version, or if it can, the new version may run very slowly. Things such as existing disk space, RAM (random access memory), processing speed, type of video card, and versions of your other (Microsoft and non-Microsoft) softwares must be taken into consideration.

Sometimes it's better to buy a new PC, rather than spend time and money trying to make yours work, especially if you plan to keep adding new software or hardware, or if your computer is more than three years old. Whether you upgrade your existing PC and version of Windows or purchase a new PC with a newer version of Windows, you may find that some or all of your other software programs will also require an upgrade to run properly. This may cost more money, so you'll want to look at these things before making a decision.

If you're considering upgrading, go to *http://windows.microsoft.com/ en-US/windows/downloads/upgrade-advisor* on the Internet to find out if your PC can run the new version. You can download and install the upgrade advisor software and it will check your system and let you know if you'll have any hardware problems or compatibility issues. You may also need to contact the manufacturers (or go to the websites) of your non-Microsoft software programs to make sure those programs will work with the new version of Windows.

Which version do you have?

To see which version of Windows you have, right-click on *Computer* on your desktop (or click on the Start button and right-click on *Computer*).

When the pull-down menu opens, move your mouse up or down to highlight *Properties* and click. The information in the rectangle in Fig. 4-1 shows the version of Windows. Service Pack number is listed below the version. Other important information is also listed here.

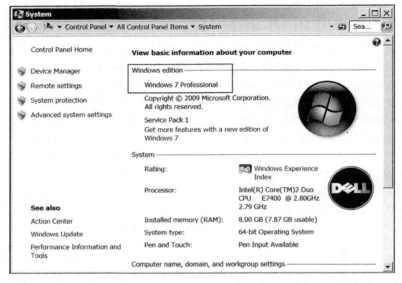

Fig. 4-1. Properties for *Computer* showing the version of Windows.

Beginning with Vista, the Windows Experience Index (WEI) has been reported in the Computer Properties menu. With my Vista laptop my WEI is 1.0, which is the lowest (5.0 is highest). This means I won't be able to use—to the fullest or perhaps at all—some of Vista's features, such as the Windows Aero or the multi-media features that would be functional with a higher WEI.

In Windows 7 the WEI is under System information. My desktop PC's WEI is 4.0 (see Fig. 4-1). If your window says the rating is not available, click on the link to go to the next window where you can rate your computer. Check the WEI on PCs at the store before you buy.

Other information for your PC includes the type of processor, amount of random access memory (RAM), graphics, gaming graphics, and primary hard disk data transfer rate. You can get explanations of those ratings or click on other links to learn how to improve the performance of your computer. Click on each link to read the information. Click *Cancel* when you're finished.

5 - Starting Up Windows

Starting up/Logging on

When you turn on your PC, one of the following things will happen, depending on your Windows version, the manufacturer of your PC, and the way your PC was set up.

(1) The Windows Desktop will appear, icons and toolbars will load, and the cursor for your mouse will show up. In this case, you're set to go, OR

(2) A "welcome" screen will appear with one or more user names. Click in the password field under your user name and type in your password, then press *Enter* or click *OK*. If you just bought the computer and haven't set up a password, then type the word *Administrator* into the account field, leave the password field blank, and click *OK*. Or click on the Guest account and hit *Enter* without putting in a password, OR

(3) A window may pop up that says "Press Ctrl-Alt-Delete to begin." Press and hold down the Ctrl key, press and also hold down the Alt key, press the Delete key (see below) and then let go of all three keys. A login window will ask for a user name and password. Then follow as above.

Fig. 5-1. The approximate locations of the Ctrl-Alt-Delete keys.

On laptops, the Delete key may be located on the bottom right of the keyboard or the upper right area or maybe somewhere else. Just look for it.

6 - The Desktop

Customizing your Desktop

To change your settings, set your *theme* first because that selection has a domino effect which extends to the Start menu, the taskbar, and the windows and their contents.

Windows 7 allows you to define your own theme and give it a name. With previous versions, you can change properties of a theme and then continue using it as a "modified" version of that particular theme.

To select a Desktop theme:

1. Right-click on your desktop to open the Desktop menu. Click on a choice that makes sense for customizing your desktop. In XP that will be *Properties,* and the Display Properties window will open as in Fig. 6-1. In Windows 7 you'll click on *Personalize.*

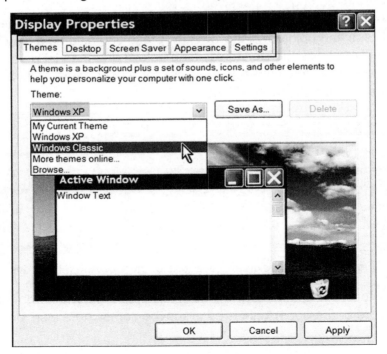

Fig. 6-1. Desktop Properties menu (XP) Themes tab.

2.   Look for *Themes*. In XP, once you're in the Properties menu, click on the tab *Themes* and your choices will be on a drop-down menu (see Fig. 6-1). In Windows 7, when you click on *Personalize,* the themes will be displayed as thumbnails (see Fig. 6-2).

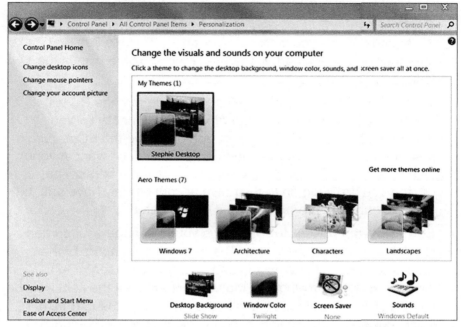

Fig. 6-2. *Personalization* window in Windows 7. "Stephie Desktop" (the only theme listed in the top section called *My Themes)* is the selected theme.

3.   When you've selected your theme, click on other items you want to change. In XP these will be on the other tabs of the Desktop Properties menu. In Windows 7 they are in the Personalization window where the themes are located but they are along the bottom of the window and in the left sidebar.

I've listed some of these customization choices below. In each case, where there's a difference between versions, I've listed the **XP name/Windows 7 name** (Vista is usually the same as Windows 7).

•   **Desktop/Desktop Background** allows you to change the Desktop background to a different color or background picture. Windows has plenty of choices available. You can also pick your own image or set up a slide show of images. Figs. 6-3 and 6-4 show how I set up a slide show for my desktop background.

- **Appearance/Window Color** allows you to change the colors of the windows.

- **Sounds** (Windows 7) allows you to change or set sounds for Low Battery Alarm, New Mail Notification, etc. (Note: XP sounds aren't changed from the Desktop Properties windows; go to *Start > Control Panel > Sounds and Audio Devices Properties* to change XP sounds. While you're there, click on the Volume Tab and make sure there's a checkmark in the box "Place volume icon in the taskbar.")

- **Screen Saver** allows you to select an image that the PC will switch to after a certain number of minutes of inactivity. You decide on the number of minutes. You can have the PC require a password to resume regular operation, if you don't want anyone else messing with your stuff while you're taking a break. The person could still log on to their own account if they have one, but your account and programs would be protected.

- **Settings/Adjust Resolution** allows you to change your screen resolution and the size of text. The higher the numbers of the resolution, the more items you can see on the screen or in a window without scrolling, but that also means that the items will be smaller. The XP *Settings* tab is in the Properties menu (Fig. 6-1); in Windows 7, click *Display* in the left sidebar of the Personalization menu (Fig. 6-2) and then click *Adjust Resolution* on the left sidebar near the top, OR right-click on a Windows 7 desktop and choose *Screen Resolution.*

Your resolution setting may be in the form of a slider bar that you drag to a higher or smaller resolution, or it may be a drop-down menu to click on. If you change the setting, click **Apply** to see what it looks like. You can cancel if you don't like it.

Also in the XP Settings menu is a button called **Advanced**. This is the same as the **Display** button in Windows 7. This setting allows you to keep the resolution you've set for your PC, but increases the size of the label/menu text and icons by 25% (all versions) or 50% (Windows 7 only). You may be told to restart your PC after choosing this setting.

To make *my* customized theme, I started out by selecting the Windows 7 Aero theme, and then made these changes.

1.   I clicked on **Window Color** in the bottom row of Fig. 6-2 and selected the darker blue for my window colors. I clicked on *Save Changes* and the window closed, taking me back to the Personalization window, but now it showed that I had changed the default Windows 7 theme to an "Unsaved Theme."

2.   I clicked on **Desktop Background**, also in the bottom row of Fig. 6-2 so that I could change the background to a slide show using pictures I had placed in a folder. See Fig. 6-3.

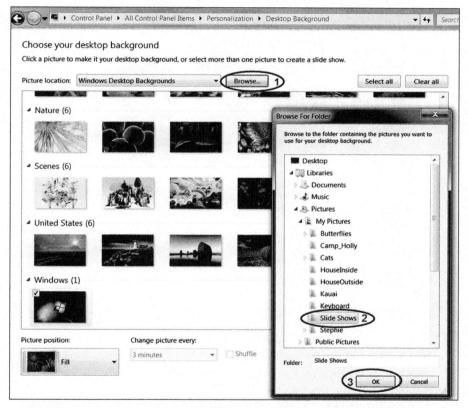

Fig. 6-3. Setting up a slide show for your desktop background (Windows 7).

Once I was in the Desktop background window shown in Fig. 6-3:

[1]   I clicked on *Browse* to look for the folder with my pictures in it (see Chapter 11 to learn how to browse).

[2]   I clicked on the *Slide Shows* folder which I had placed inside My Pictures folder.

[3]   I clicked OK**.**

Now Windows knows to use this folder of pictures for a Desktop background slide show, but it gives me some more options to decide on. See Fig. 6-4.

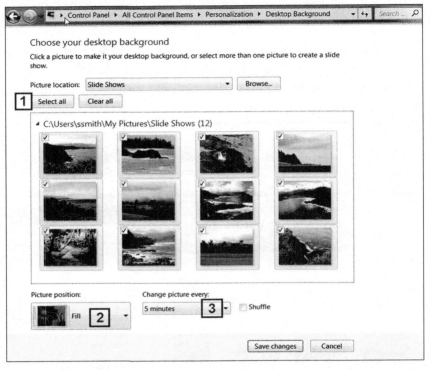

Fig. 6-4. Options for the Desktop background slide show (Windows 7).

In the "Choose your desktop background" window:

[1] I clicked on *Select all* to select all pictures in the folder for the slide show. If there were any I didn't want to include, I could click the box on those pictures to uncheck them.

[2] I selected the way I want the pictures to appear on the screen (Fit, Fill, Stretch, Tile, Center) by clicking the drop-down menu arrow under *Picture position*.

[3] I clicked on the drop-down menu under *Change picture every* and selected the number of minutes I want between the slide changes. I could have also clicked in the box next to *Shuffle*, and Windows would randomly select pictures to display.

When I finished making these selections, I clicked on *Save changes* at the bottom. The window closed, putting me back at the Personal-ization window where I clicked on *Save Theme* at the top to the right of my Unnamed Theme, and I gave the new theme a name.

Recycle Bin

The Recycle Bin (Fig. 6-5) will be on your desktop. When you delete something—a file, folder, picture, icon—it goes into the Recycle Bin, where it stays until you delete it from there, which deletes it from the PC. To see what's in the Bin, just open it.

Recycle Bin

Fig. 6-5. The Recycle Bin icon on the desktop (XP).

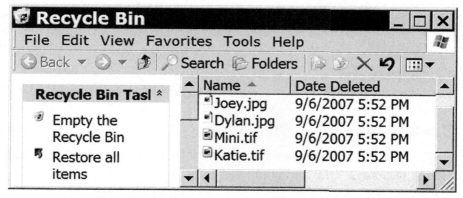

Fig. 6-6. The opened Recycle Bin folder with the contents displayed in *Details* view (XP).

There are several ways **to put an item in your Recycle Bin**:

(1)   Click on the item and press the Delete key, OR
(2)   Drag the item and drop it in the Recycle Bin, OR
(3)   Right-click on the item and select *Cut*, then open the Recycle Bin, right-click in an empty area and select *Paste*.

The items in your Recycle Bin take up hard disk space, so if you need space, delete items you know you don't want. Otherwise, leave them in the Bin; Windows will eventually delete them.

To delete all items from your Recycle Bin:

(1) Right-click on the Recycle Bin and choose *Empty the Recycle Bin,* OR

(2) Open the Recycle Bin and if you have a Task Pane showing at the left of the folder (as in Fig. 6-6 showing an XP window), click on *Empty the Recycle Bin* there (in Windows 7, that option is at the top of the window), OR

(3) Open the Recycle Bin, press Ctrl+A to select all items and press delete.

To **restore a Recycle Bin item** back to where it was before you deleted it:

(1) Right-click on the item in the bin and click *Restore,* OR

(2) Select the item and click *Restore* in the Recycle Bin folder's task pane, OR

(3) Select the item and click on the Recycle Bin's File menu and click *Restore*, OR

(4) You can also drag the item out of the bin and into any folder or onto your desktop.

As I keep pointing out, there are several ways to accomplish the same task. Try them all to discover the most efficient way to work.

Customizing your Start Menu

The Start button/Windows Orb is located to the far left of the taskbar. This button says "Start" in some versions and themes; in others it doesn't. The various versions of Windows have slightly different looking Start menus. All Start menus do the same things and pretty much make the same items available.

The below list corresponds to the numbers in Fig. 6-7.

[1] Shows the User Name.

[2] These are programs I use a lot, so I've "pinned" them to my Start menu for easy access.

[3] These are programs that pinned themselves to my Start menu because I have it set up to automatically pin recently used or newly installed programs to the menu.

[4] The "main" items that Windows placed here. You can make changes to this area.

[5] Click on or mouse over *All Programs* and a menu will appear with a list of all programs on your PC.

[6] The area where you log off, shut down, restart, etc.

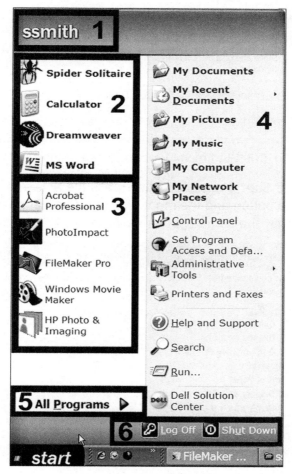

Fig. 6-7. Start menu (XP).

To customize your Start menu, right-click on the Start button and click on *Properties*. The *Taskbar and Start Menu Properties* menu will open with the Start menu as the active tab since you're clicking from the Start menu.

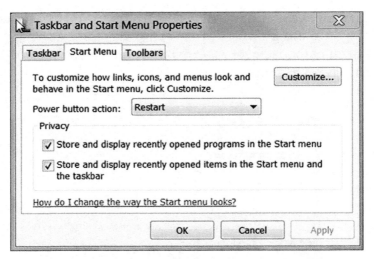

Fig. 6-8. Start menu Properties Tab (Windows 7).

In Fig. 6-8, the Start menu properties tab is the active tab. Click on the *Customize* button and the menu in Fig. 6-9 will appear. Windows XP has basically the same options as Windows 7.

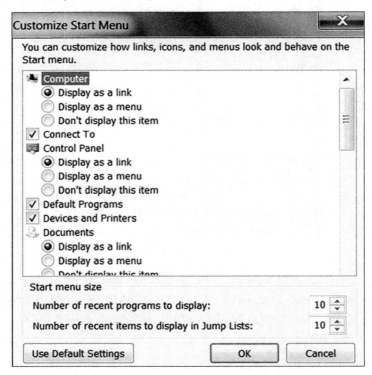

Fig. 6-9. The Start menu's *Customize* menu (Windows 7).

If you set items to **"Display as a link"** on your Start menu, a separate window containing the folders, subfolders, and files will open. If you choose to **"Display as a menu,"** a cascading menu pops up showing you the first level of folders; move your mouse over one of those folders, and its subfolders and/or files will pop-up. Try setting all the options to either link or menu except one and then check out the difference to see which you prefer.

You can "pin" or unpin items to your Start menu. Windows has already pinned some, but you can remove them: right-click on the item on the Start menu and choose "remove from this list."

To place another program on your Start menu, click on *Start*, point to *All Programs*, find the program, right-click, and *Pin to Start menu*. Pinning is available for programs, but not folders or files. To add a folder or file, you'll need to create a shortcut, and then drag the shortcut to your Start button or Start menu. See "Creating Shortcuts to Programs, Folders, or Files" in Chapter 11.

Customizing your Taskbar

The taskbar is the management area of your desktop. It's usually along the bottom of your screen, but you can drag it to the top or either side. All open programs, folders, files, or windows show up on the taskbar.

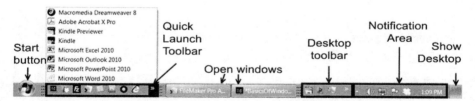

Fig. 6-10. Various components of the Taskbar, including the Start button (to the far left), which opens the Start Menu.

To the right of the Start button will be the Quick Launch toolbar, if applicable (Windows 7 did away with it). Open windows will be docked along the center of the taskbar. The System Tray/Notification Area will be to the right of that. (See "System Tray/Notification Area on the Taskbar" later in this chapter.)

All open items will show on the taskbar. **If the taskbar becomes crowded, here are some things you can do:**

(1) **Turn off the Quick Launch toolbar**, remove unnecessary items, or resize it to make it smaller (see "Quick Launch Toolbar on the Taskbar" on the next page), OR

(2) **Remove or hide unnecessary items from the System/Notification** area (see System Tray/Notification Area), OR

(3) **Increase the taskbar height** by dragging the top of the taskbar upward (in Fig. 6-12, I increased the taskbar height to show two rows), OR

(4) **Group or combine similar items together.** Right-click on an empty area of the taskbar and select *Properties*. In the Properties window: in XP and Vista click the box that says *Group similar [items or taskbar buttons];* in Windows 7, click the drop-down menu for "Taskbar buttons" and set the taskbar to "Always combine, hide labels" or "Combine when taskbar is full."

Grouping similar items this way will result in all Internet Explorer web pages being grouped under one taskbar button, all Word documents being grouped under one button, etc. When you click on the group button on the taskbar, the list or thumbnails of the grouped items will pop up. Move your mouse up to highlight the one you want and click on it. That window will be restored to the desktop or, if the window is already open on the desktop, the window will move to the front of the other windows.

Fig. 6-11. Grouped Internet Explorer thumbnails that popped up when I moused over the IE icon on the Taskbar (Windows 7).

Figs. 6-12 and 6-13 were taken on the same day at the same PC with the same version of Windows, so why does the taskbar look so different? It's because in the first picture the PC is set to the Windows XP theme and in the second, it's set to the Windows Classic theme. Changing the theme changes the look of everything.

Fig. 6-12. XP Professional Taskbar (XP Theme)

Fig. 6-13. XP Professional Taskbar (Windows Classic Theme).

In any version of Windows, you can drag most items around within an area of your taskbar. Just drag the icon to the location you want it. A horizontal line with show up in the position where the item will go if you release your mouse button at that time. If the line isn't where you want it, keep dragging the item until it is. Then let go.

Quick Launch Toolbar on the Taskbar

In Vista and XP, the icons directly to the right of the Start button belong to the Quick Launch (QL) toolbar. Windows 7 did away with this toolbar and instead combines the program icons and the open windows together on the taskbar. I didn't like the result (program icons and open windows are all mixed together), so I reinstalled my QL toolbar.

The **QL toolbar gives you one-click access to the Internet and other programs** you add to it, just as the regular taskbar in Windows 7 does. You can turn the toolbar off if you want more room on the taskbar for your open windows.

Fig. 6-14. Windows Quick Launch toolbar (XP) with chevron displayed.

You can also shrink the QL toolbar down so that only a couple of icons are showing as in Figs. 6-14 and 6-15. Whenever there are **two small arrows (called chevron) pointing to the right of a toolbar** on the taskbar, it means more items are available if you click. So, click on the chevron and a menu will appear showing the other programs (see Fig. 6-15). You can then click on the program you want to open.

Fig. 6-15. QL toolbar (reinstalled) in Windows 7. I clicked on the chevron to show all items on the QL toolbar since only four icons show on the taskbar.

To see all the icons on the toolbar instead of looking at them on a pop-up menu, expand the toolbar area. Just move your mouse pointer over the divider bar until it turns into a two-header pointer (see Figs. 6-16 and 6-17), and then drag to the right until the chevron disappears.

Fig. 6-16. Two-headed arrow over divider bar (XP Theme).
In this theme the divider bar is a double dotted line.

Fig. 6-17. Two-headed arrow over divider bar (XP Classic Theme).
In this theme the divider bar is one solid line.

If you're not sure your QL toolbar is showing, right-click on an empty spot on the taskbar. When the taskbar menu appears, click on *Toolbars* (left side of Fig. 6-18) to open the Toolbars menu (right side of Fig. 6-18). If your QL toolbar is open, there will be a checkmark next to it. To turn it off, click on the checkmark. The checkmark will disappear and so will the toolbar.

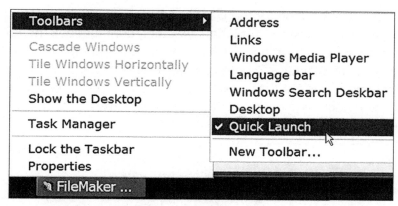

Fig. 6-18. The checkmark next to "Quick Launch" shows
that the QL toolbar is turned on (XP).

System Tray/Notification Area on the Taskbar

The group of icons to the far right of the taskbar is called the **Notification Area—referred to as the System Tray in earlier versions
of Windows** (see Fig. 6-19.) This area shows connected hardware
(flash drive, digital camera, MP3 player) or programs that are running
in the background, such as Internet or network connections, virus
software, and printer. To access one of those items, click on the
program's icon. The speaker volume control (looks like a horn) is
here; click on it to drag the volume up and down.

Fig. 6-19. Notification Area (XP Professional).

You can decide which icons to show in your Notification Area
by clicking on the *Customize* button for the Notification Area. In
Windows 7 and Vista, you can also get to the Customize menu by
clicking on the arrow to the left of the Notification Area. Once there,
decide which icons you want to always appear, which ones you want
to appear only when there is a notification, etc.

On the right side of the Notification Area is the clock. To set time and
date or to look at the calendar, double click on the time in XP (single
click in Vista and Windows 7). Mouse over the clock to see the day
and date.

Vista also has a button for the **Desktop Sidebar,** which displays a collection of "**Gadgets**" (notepad, weather, contact book, headlines, stocks, etc.). Windows 7 has Gadgets too, but they are not on the taskbar. In Windows 7, right-click on your desktop and click on *Gadgets* for access to these items. You can click on an item in the Gadgets window and click on "Show details" (lower left corner of Fig. 6-20).

Fig. 6-20. Gadgets window in Windows 7.

You can drag **a copy** of the item out of the gadgets window to place on your desktop. Then mouse over the icon to see what pops up in the upper right corner of the gadget. There may be an arrow that allows you to make the gadget larger, or a wrench which allows you to set options. You can also right-click on the gadget to choose options such as "Always on top" which makes the gadget show on top of open windows, or you can click on the X (Close) to remove the gadget from your desktop. XP doesn't have Gadgets.

In the Windows 7 Notification Area, there's another improvement called the **Action Center, represented by a white flag**. If there's a red X over the flag, something is wrong. Hover over the white flag and a message will pop up to tell you the problem.

In Fig. 6-21, there was no red X signifying an actual problem, but when I moused over the white flag, a pop-up message told me there were two PC issues. If you get a pop-up message, click on the white flag to read it. To resolve the problem(s), follow the prompts.

You can set up your Windows updates to install automatically or manually through the Action Center. If you choose to do it manually, don't forget. Many of the updates pertain to security issues.

Fig. 6-21. Action Center on the taskbar (Windows 7 only).

On the far right side of the Windows 7 taskbar is the *Show Desktop* area. See the section called "Show Desktop" in Chapter 7 for more about this.

Taskbar Properties

Right-click on the taskbar and click on *Properties.* The Properties menu that pops up is the same Properties menu that you opened to customize your Start menu, only this time, because you are opening the menu from the taskbar, the Taskbar tab is the active tab. In Windows 7 there will also be a third tab for Toolbars.

The choices are slightly different for the taskbar properties in the various versions of Windows. Take a look at each option on your menu and click or unclick the checkboxes. You can click *Apply* to see the changes as you make them. If you don't like the change, just switch back.

In addition to checkboxes, there may also be drop-down menus with choices, as in Fig. 6-22, which has drop-down menus for the Taskbar location and Taskbar buttons.

In Windows 7, the third tab allows you to **add toolbars to your taskbar.** You can also add them by right-clicking on the taskbar, highlighting *Toolbars* so that the drop-down menu opens, and clicking on the toolbars you want to add. Or add a toolbar for an important folder by clicking on *New Toolbar* and browsing to and choosing the folder. I added a toolbar for my Desktop so that I can click to open an item on my desktop directly from my Taskbar without closing or manipulating any of the open windows.

Fig. 6-22. Taskbar Properties Menu Tab (Windows 7).

You can **add programs to your taskbar** in a couple of ways. With Windows 7 you can find the program on the Start menu, right-click and choose *Pin to Taskbar*. In any version of Windows, you can put a shortcut to the program on your desktop, and then drag it onto the taskbar.

Once the taskbar is set up the way you want it, lock it in place by checking *Lock the Taskbar*. To make changes after that, you'll have to unlock the taskbar first, but you may find it worth that extra trouble.

7 - The Window

What is a Window?

A window is a framed view of a file, a folder (collection of files), or an application (software program). When you open a file, folder, or application, it opens up in a window on your desktop.

Several windows can be open at once but only one window can be active at a time. In XP, the active window will look different from the other windows that are open on your screen, just as a selected desktop icon or selected file in a folder will look different. It may have a different color scheme or the colors may be stronger. And if windows are overlapping, then the active window will always be the one on top.

Fig. 7-1. Selected Windows (XP). *Kauai* is selected on the left; *My Computer* is selected on the right.

With Vista, you can only tell the active window by one small detail: the little square containing the X in the upper right corner of the window. If the window is active, that square will be red. If it's not active, the square will be blue. If you use the standard Vista theme, you can't change this. Windows 7 is the same as Vista except the title bar of the active window is slightly darker than the others.

The Parts of a Window

The parts of a window will vary, depending on your version of Windows and whether that window contains a folder, a file, a menu, or an application. These differences are discussed in Chapter 10.

But all windows have some things in common because we have to be able to close them, make them smaller and larger, move them around, and learn certain information about them. So there are some parts that show up in every window, regardless of what that window contains. Fig. 7-2 is a screen shot of an XP folder that shows some of those parts.

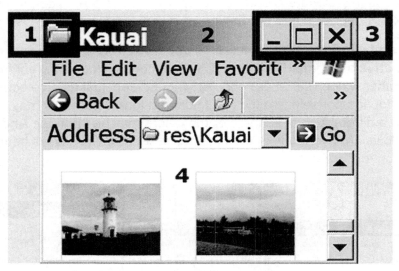

Fig. 7-2. An Open Folder (XP).

[1] **Icon tells you what the window is,** in this case a folder.
[2] **Title bar usually gives the name of the window** and is also the area where you click to drag a window.
[3] **These icons minimize, maximize, restore, and close the window.** (Note: The Restore button doesn't show in this picture. See Fig. 7-4 to view all four buttons.)
[4] **The items the window contains,** in this case, photos taken in Kaua'i. This folder is set to Thumbnail view so that I can view the photos.

Vista and Windows 7 folders have a title bar, but the title doesn't show if you're using the default theme. However, the address bar will show you what folder you're in. The address bar in Fig. 7-3 shows that I'm in the folder called Essays, which is a folder inside the Documents folder. To learn about file and folder paths, see Chapter 11.

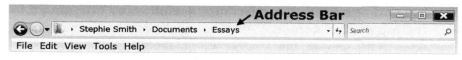

Fig. 7-3. Folder Address Bar (Vista).

Minimize, Maximize, Restore, and Close

In the upper right corner of a window are three small icons or symbols. Each represents a different function. *Minimize* and *Close* will always show in this area. The middle button, however, will show *Maximize* **OR** *Restore* but never both.

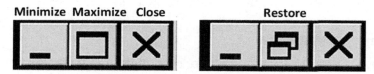

Fig. 7-4. A window's Minimize, Maximize, Restore, and Close icons.

- *Minimize* is the button with the icon that looks like a hyphen. When you click on the *Minimize* button, the window disappears from your desktop, but you can see it on your taskbar because it's still running. Minimize a window when you aren't using it or it's in your way but you plan to use it again. When you're ready to use the window again, click on it on the taskbar. The window will go back to its previous location on your desktop.

- *Maximize* is the button that looks like a square. Clicking on this enlarges the window to fill the screen for easier viewing.

- *Restore* looks like a double square. Click on *Restore* to change the full-size window back to the size and location it was before you maximized it. The double square will then change back to the single square (Maximize) in the top right corner of the window.

- *Close* is the button that looks like an X. It closes the window completely so it's no longer running. Click on this when you're finished with a window. Anther way to close a window is to right-click on the window on the taskbar and click on the X.

Here are other ways to maximize, minimize, or restore windows.

(1) In any version of Windows, **double-click a window's title bar to maximize the window**. Double-click again to restore it back to the size and location it was, OR

(2) **In Windows 7, you can maximize a window by dragging it to the top of your screen**. When the mouse pointer touches the edge of the screen, the window will maximize. Drag the window back down to restore it, OR

(3) Also **in Windows 7, you can minimize all but one window by clicking in the title bar and shaking that window back and forth** a couple of times. The other windows will minimize to your taskbar, leaving only that one window open on your Desktop. Note that this will not maximize the window or change its position in any other way. To bring back the other windows to your desktop, shake the same window back and forth again.

Moving a Window

To move a window from one place to another in any version of Windows:

1. **Click on an empty part of the title bar and hold down the mouse button.** As mentioned, Vista and Windows 7 title bars may not show the title, depending on the theme you've chosen, but you still click on the area known as the title bar to drag the window.
2. **Drag the window to its new location.**
3. **Release the mouse button.**

Fig. 7-5. A title bar's empty area where you click to "drag."

Now you know how to minimize, maximize, close, restore, and move windows, but there are other ways to manipulate them too.

Resizing a Window

To resize a window to make room for another one on your desktop:

1. Move your mouse pointer slowly over the window frame—any corner, either side, the top, or bottom of the window, depending on how you want to resize the window—until **the pointer turns into a two-headed arrow** as in the rectangle in Fig. 7-6.

2. **Resize by dragging** (one click with mouse button held down) and pulling the frame to the size you want.

3. **Release the mouse button**.

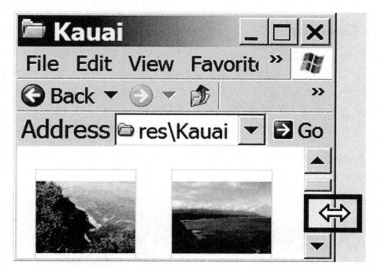

Fig. 7-6. The double-headed arrow allows you to resize a window.

- Resizing from the sides changes the window's width (Fig. 7-6).
- Resizing from the top or bottom changes the window's height.
- Resizing from a corner changes the height and width together (Fig. 7-7).

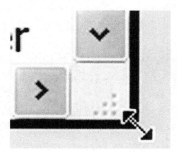

Fig. 7-7. Resizing a window's height and width at the same time.

In Fig. 7-7, dragging diagonally *toward* the middle of the window will decrease the window's height and width. Dragging *away from* the window will increase its height and width.

Note that the two-headed arrow in Fig. 7-6 looks different from the one in Fig. 7-7, even though this is the same Windows XP Professional laptop set up with the same overall theme. That's because I chose a different mouse pointer theme for the second picture.

There are still other ways to manipulate windows.

Show Desktop

Sometimes you want to get to your desktop but it's filled with open windows. The taskbar has a feature called *Show Desktop* that allows you to do this. In XP (Fig. 7-8) and Vista (Fig. 7-9), *Show Desktop* is an icon on your QL toolbar; in Windows 7 (Fig. 7-10) it's an empty rectangle located on the far right side of the taskbar.

***Show Desktop* minimizes all your open windows to the Taskbar but leaves them running.**

Fig. 7-8. Show Desktop icon (XP).

Fig. 7-9. Show Desktop (Vista).

Fig. 7-10. Show Desktop (Windows 7).

In Windows 7 it works the same way with one additional feature, if you're using a *Windows Aero* desktop theme. In that case **you can preview your desktop (called Aero Peek) by mousing over the *Show Desktop* area.** The open windows will disappear, leaving only their outlines, but once you move the mouse pointer away, the windows will reappear. If you want to minimize those windows to your taskbar, you have to actually click on Show Desktop.

Another way to show your desktop in any version of Windows is to right-click on an **empty area** of the taskbar and choose *Show the Desktop* from the menu that opens (Fig. 7-11).

In Windows 7 you can also see the items on your desktop by installing the Desktop toolbar on your taskbar as mentioned in Chapter 6.

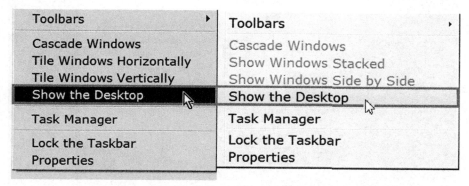

Fig. 7-11. XP Menu (left) and Vista/Windows 7 Menu (right).

Finding a Window

If you have several windows open and can't find the one you're looking for, try this: **hold down the Alt key and press the Tab key repeatedly** until you tab to the window you want. Then let go of both keys and the window will appear on top of the others.

Windows 7 has a new feature called Windows Flip; it's an *Aero* theme feature, so you must be using an Aero theme for Windows Flip to work. **Press the Windows logo key (also called Windows Orb) plus the Tab key** to make the windows stack on the desktop. If you keep both keys pressed down, all the windows will rotate past your view. Or, once the windows start scrolling, let go of just the Tab key to stop the rotation. Press the Tab key repeatedly (while still holding down the ORB) to see each window move to the front. When you see the window you want, let go of both keys and that window will be on top.

The Aero Flip picture in Fig. 7-12 was taken with a camera, since I wasn't able to take it as a screen shot. I covered the desktop background picture due to possible copyright infringement.

Fig. 7-12. Windows Aero Flip lets you see all windows
on your desktop open at once (Windows 7 only).

Arranging all Windows at once

Still more ways to manipulate your open windows …

Right-click on the taskbar for the menus shown in Fig. 7-13. The XP
taskbar menu is shown on the left; Windows 7/Vista is on the right.

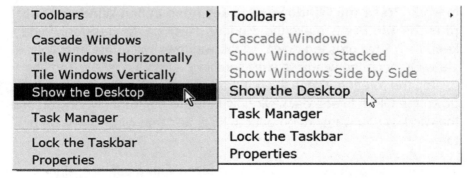

Fig. 7-13. The taskbar's right-click menu shows more ways to manipulate
the windows. These options are the same but with slightly different wording.

Tile Windows Horizontally/Show Windows Stacked. Select this to stack your open windows, one on top of the other. Only windows that are actually showing on the desktop will be stacked, i.e., those that are minimized to the taskbar will not be included. Use this option to compare contents of open folders or for copying and pasting information between them.

Tile Windows Vertically/Show Windows Side By Side. Select this to place your open windows side by side.

Choosing either of the above will result in the windows filling your screen. *Cascade Windows* is the only choice that will show all open windows while leaving a bit of your desktop showing. Do this if you need access to your desktop but don't want to minimize everything to the taskbar. (Note: On one of my XP computers, I can choose *Cascade Windows* with a right click. On the other I must click with the left button. Do whatever works.)

If menu items are grayed out, they aren't available as choices. This is true of any menu in any version of Windows. In Fig. 7-13, *Cascade Windows*, *Show Windows Stacked*, and *Show Windows Side by Side* in the Windows 7 taskbar menu on the right are grayed out because there were no open windows to manipulate.

In Windows 7 there's a new way to view *two* windows side by side. Drag one window to the left and the other window to the right. In each case, when your mouse touches the side of the screen, the window will expand to fill that half of the screen. If you have more than two windows to view, you'll need to follow the instructions in the previous paragraph or resize individually.

Scrolling to see a Window's Contents

Sometimes a window isn't large enough to show all its contents, even if you maximize the window to full view. In that case, scroll bars will show up automatically so that you can scroll the window's contents past your view. As items scroll out of your view, they disappear under the window frame but are still there.

The window in Fig. 7-14 is neither wide enough nor tall enough to show all the information it contains, so both vertical and horizontal scroll bars are present.

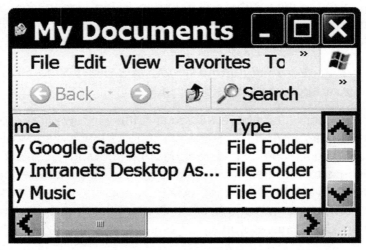

Fig. 7-14. XP Window with both vertical and horizontal scroll bars.

In Fig. 7-15, the window has no scroll bars. This tells you all the contents of the window are showing.

Fig. 7-15. XP Window without Scroll Bars.

If your mouse has a thumbwheel, you can use it to scroll up and down inside a window. Just click on an empty area inside the window first to activate the window. You can also use your keyboard arrow keys to scroll a selected window.

Using Scroll Bars

To scroll a window:

[1] Click on the up arrow to see items hidden in the top of the window.

[2] Click on the slider (the solid part) and drag it up or down (or left or right, if it's a horizontal scroll bar). Release the mouse button when items are where you want them.

[3] Click on the down arrow to see items hidden in the bottom of the window.

[4] Click on the depressed parts (see Fig. 7-17) to make the slider bar move incrementally in the direction you click.

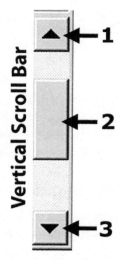

Fig. 7-16. Vertical scroll bars appear when the window is not *tall* enough to show all the items.

Horizontal scrolling works the same way. Just click on the arrow pointing right to see items hidden to the right, etc.

Horizontal Scroll Bar

Fig. 7-17. Horizontal scroll bars appear when a window isn't *wide* enough to show all the items.

Also, there may be more than one scroll bar in a window; Facebook is an example where there's a main window that you scroll vertically and then a news feed with a separate scrollbar.

Okay. You've learned that to see items in a window you can maximize or resize the window until the scroll bars disappear, or leave the window alone and just scroll to see the contents. Other choices for folder views are covered in Chapter 10.

Now, go to Chapter 13 and try Exercises 1 and 2.

8 - Shutting Down Windows

The Start Button is also the Stop button. Whenever you shut down your PC, you should try to do it from the Start button so that Windows can shut down properly. This may preclude some unexpected problems upon restarting.

Shutting down XP

When I click on the Start button, both my XP Home Edition and XP Professional show the Shut Down options below (see Fig. 8-1).

Fig. 8-1. Shutting Down (XP).

But once I click on *Shut Down*, I get a different menu from my two PCs. XP Home has a menu that says "Turn Off Computer" with four choices: *Stand By, Turn Off, Restart and Cancel.* XP Professional gives me the menu in Fig. 8-2 below. I click on the drop-down menu, click on my choice and click *OK*.

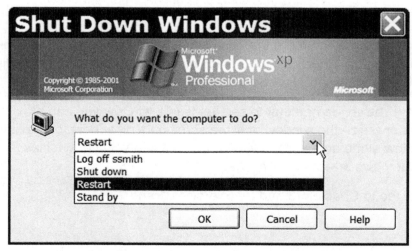

Fig. 8-2. The Shut-down Menu (XP Professional).

Some PCs go to a screen that says, "It is now safe to turn off your Computer." Then you press the power button to turn off the PC.

Shutting down Vista

Vista gives you more options for shutting down. And unlike XP, Vista (and Windows 7) won't ask if you're sure or bring up a second screen where you have the chance to cancel your action. When you click the Vista Start button, you'll see the 3 buttons in the rectangle in Fig. 8-3. The button on the left puts the PC in sleep mode or turns it off, depending on whether that circle is broken (sleep mode) or not (off). The middle button locks it. The right button opens a pull-down menu that includes those same two choices plus others (Fig. 8-4).

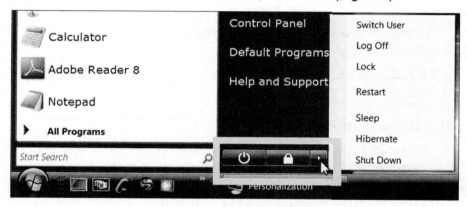

Fig. 8-3. Shut-down buttons (Vista).

Fig. 8-4. Shut-down Menu (Vista) that appears when I click on the button on the right of the rectangle in Fig. 8-3.

- **Switch User** lets you **switch to another user** but keeps your stuff open and ready for you.

- **Log Off** logs you off and returns to the Welcome screen, but leaves the PC on.

- **Lock** locks the PC in case you leave for a while and don't want anyone messing with it.

- **Restart** will shut the PC down and restart it. Do this when Windows is acting weird or when it tells you to, e.g., you've installed something new.

- **Sleep** saves your work and puts PC in **Sleep mode**. Press the Power button briefly to turn PC back on with everything the way you left it.

- **Hibernate** saves your work and turns the PC off (takes more power than Sleep).

- **Shut Down** shuts the PC down. You'll be asked to save work if needed.

Shutting down Windows 7

To shut down a Windows 7 PC, click on the "Shut Down" button on the bottom right of the Start menu. A few of the previously mentioned options are available there too by clicking on the arrow. You can customize the Start menu properties to put *Shut Down* or *Restart* here by default. See Chapter 6, "Customizing Your Start menu."

Shutting down any PC

Everyone has a theory about whether or not to shut down a PC when it's not in use. Some think you should leave it running so Windows can perform maintenance and other system tasks such as automatic updates. Some think you should turn it off to save power and life of hardware components. I think if your PC is on long enough (when you do have it on) for Windows to perform the needed tasks, you can do whatever you want. By "long enough" I'm talking 15 minutes, because that gives Windows time to start and finish a task. If Windows *does* start a task and you try to shut down in the middle of it, Windows will let you know. Still not sure? Then shut it down in between uses if you don't know how good your firewall and virus softwares are, especially if you're connected to the Internet. Definitely shut down during lightning storms, if the computer is not protected from power surge.

If you don't shut down periodically, it's a good idea to Restart your PC once a week so that Windows can clear out memory and tempo-rary files. This is especially true if you use the Internet. Restarting your PC also allows Windows to check its system files and make sure everything is running correctly. Restarting your PC about once a week will help your PC run faster and more efficiently. If Windows has installed an update, it might restart your PC for you if you've chosen to let Windows install updates automatically.

When you shut down your computer, other hardware components may or may not shut down too. If your monitor (screen) doesn't turn off automatically, it may go into a sleep mode. Touching your mouse will turn the screen back on.

Mom and Her New PC

I called Mom to tell her I was giving her a Windows PC. She immediately began to fret. "Will they be able to see me, or will I just be able to see them?" she asked.

"Who?"

"*Them*. The people on the other side of the windows. Will they watch me while I'm sleeping? I can't stand for anyone to watch me while I'm sleeping."

"It's a computer," I said. "It doesn't have real windows."

"Then why do they call it *Windows?*"

"Well, there *are* windows, but they're not for watching people."

"Hmmph. My sister Louise watched *Oprah* through *her* computer window," she countered.

"But Oprah was not watching Louise," I replied. "Really, there's no way someone can watch you through your computer. I promise. It's just not possible."

"Then why were they talking on TV about a man who was using his computer to look up women's skirts?" she asked, her voice rising.

"That's different," I assured her. "The man must have had a camera situated near those women in order to do that."

"I have a camera!" she shrieked.

I made a noise like static and hung up the phone.

9 - Programs

An Overview of Programs, Folders, and Files

A **program** is a software application. A program usually consists of many files, but a small program may consist of just one. Windows comes with programs installed, some of which you will knowingly use (games, Internet Explorer, Wordpad, etc.), some of which you will set up and then mostly leave alone (anti-virus software, printer software), and some of which you will never see because they work in the background to keep Windows operating correctly.

A **folder** is a storage place, just like a folder in a file cabinet. Folders are used to organize and store groups of files. Windows comes with lots of folders that contain the files needed to run the Windows operating system and all its added programs.

Windows also comes with other folders that were created for you to store *your* files in, such as *My Documents* (or just *Documents*) folder, *My Pictures* folder, *My Music* folder, and so on. You should use these folders to store the items they were created for; it will save you time.

Programs are made up of **files**, but *you* can create files too. A letter saved in Microsoft Word is a file. A photo downloaded from your camera is a file. A saved spreadsheet is a file. (Actually, if you don't save it, it's still a file—a temporary file that eventually gets deleted by Windows.)

Every file you create will open into a window on your desktop. That's not necessarily true of the files Windows uses to run the PC because Windows doesn't want you opening some of those.

So, there are the Windows files and folders, and there are **your** files and folders. Until you know what you're doing, only delete files and folders that **you create**. If you delete a file you didn't create, your PC may not work correctly, or perhaps at all.

Opening Programs

Following are several different ways to open a program. Try them all.

To customize your Start menu to display some of the options mentioned below, see Chapter 6.

(1)   From the Start menu top level

Check your Start menu first for the program to see if it's there; if it is, click to open. If it's not there, you can pin it (Chapter 6) or place a shortcut (Chapter 11) there for future use. Recently used programs will show up on the Start menu after you've used them; you can customize the menu to show as many as you wish.

(2)   From the Start menu > All Programs menu

Click *Start*, then click or highlight *All Programs* (Fig. 9-1).

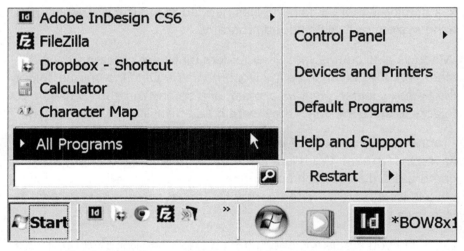

Fig. 9-1. Windows 7 *All Programs* link on the Start menu.

In XP a menu may pop up to the right; in Windows 7 or Vista, it may be a scrollable area on the Start menu (Fig. 9-2).

Some programs may be grouped together in a folder; highlight or click on that folder and any other subfolders to drill down to the program you want. In Fig. 9-2 I clicked on *All Programs* and scrolled until I saw the *Games* folder. When I moused over that, I saw two games listed. I love Spider Solitaire!

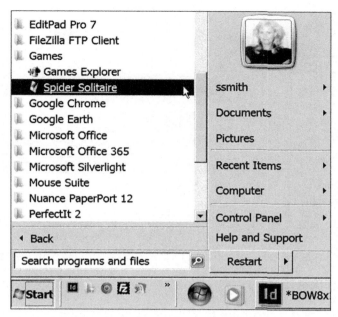

Fig. 9-2. Drilling down from All Programs and the Games folder to Spider Solitaire in Windows 7.

(3) From Recent Documents/Items

Click on the Start menu, and click on (or mouse over) *Recent Documents* (XP) or *Recent Items* (Vista, Windows 7). Click on a document that was created in the application you want to open.

For example, if you wrote a letter yesterday in Microsoft Word and you want to open Microsoft Word to type a different letter, click on *Recent Documents/Recent Items* and select the letter you typed yesterday (see Fig. 9-3). If you want your second letter to look the same as the first, choose *File > Save As* and give the letter a new name. The new letter will be saved in the same location as the previous letter, which will be unchanged. Then make your changes to the new letter and save it again.

If you want a different format for this letter, then close yesterday's letter (click Word's *File* menu, click *Close*) without exiting the program. Then open a blank file by clicking Word's *File* menu, *New* (or press Ctrl+N). You may then have to click *Create* or press *Enter* to confirm. To learn how to see where the new letter will be saved or to browse to save it somewhere else, see Chapter 11.

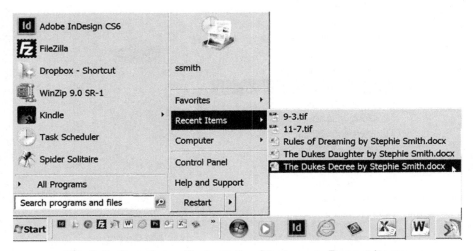

Fig. 9-3. Opening a file from the Start menu Recent Items.

(4) From the Taskbar

If you've pinned a program to your taskbar (or placed a shortcut on it), click on the program's icon on the taskbar to open it.

(5) From a shortcut you created

You can open a program from a shortcut you've placed on your desktop or somewhere else. See "Creating Shortcuts to Programs, Folders, and Files" in Chapter 11.

(6) Automatically, via the Start Up folder

If there's a program you use a lot, you can have Windows open it every time you start your PC by placing a shortcut to the program inside the *Startup* folder. Here's how:

1. Create a shortcut to the program. (See Chapter 11.)
2. Click *Start > All Programs* and look for the Startup folder.
3. Right-click and choose *Open.*
4. Drag the shortcut into the Startup folder.

Switching between and closing Programs

The easiest way to switch between programs is to click on the program's open window on the taskbar. To close the program, click the X on the window, or right-click the program name on the taskbar and click *Close Window.*

Closing a Frozen Program

At some point your PC may "freeze," which means that your mouse and keyboard won't work. People often turn off their PCs when this happens, but try these things first:

Click on a different program to see if your mouse works there. If it does, close that program and any other open applications. If windows from the same program are grouped together on the taskbar, *Close Group* instead. Sometimes a freeze can be caused by a memory problem, i.e., your PC runs out of available memory because you have so many items running, so closing extra programs may free up memory.

If you've closed all the applications you can, and the PC still isn't responding on the remaining program, open your Task Manager. To get there:

1. Right-click on the clock or the Notification Area and click on *Start Task Manager.* If that option isn't available, press your Ctrl key and hold it down, press the Alt key and hold both keys down, and press the Delete key. Release all three keys and click on *Start Task Manager.*

2. Click on the *Applications* tab. If the words "not responding" are next to a program, click on that program and click *End Task.*

3. If the PC won't let you do the above, press your Restart button if you have one. If you don't have a Restart button, press your Power button to turn the PC off, wait a few seconds after the computer has shut down, and then press the Power button to turn it back on.

Always close out any programs you can before you force a restart.

Programs installed in Windows

Each version of Windows has programs installed or available to install from your system or CDs. Microsoft.com has additional programs you can download from their website (some free, some not). You can also purchase or download other software applications as well. If you buy software online, download it only from the developer's site until you become very savvy about this topic. And never ever download software from a link in an *unsolicited* email.

Below are programs listed alphabetically that may come with your
version of Windows. I won't explain how to use most of them; you can
search for information or you can open the application and click on
the *Help* menu.

Calculator

Start > All Programs > Accessories > Calculator. Calculator is very
simple in XP; under *View* you have the choice of *Standard* or *Scientific.* In Windows 7 you have several new options. For example, you
can mouse over the *Worksheets* option and choose *Mortgage* to
calculate your monthly mortgage payment based on purchase price,
term, and interest rate.

Character Map

Start > All Programs > Accessories > System Tools > Character Map.
Use Character Map to copy and paste special characters—such as
the trademark symbol, special mathematical characters, or a symbol
from the character set of another language—into your documents.

Disk Defragmenter

Start > All Programs > Accessories > System Tools > Disk Defragmenter. Disk Defragmenter consolidates fragmented files on your
computer's hard disk to improve system performance. Click on your
hard disk and click *Analyze disk.* If the fragmentation is over 10%,
you should defragment the disk. It really does improve performance
which means your PC will run faster. The Vista and Windows 7
versions of this program can be scheduled to run at whatever time
you want; the XP version must be run manually.

Email Programs

Outlook Express is Microsoft's email program in XP. **Windows Mail**
is the email program in Vista. They are similar. The problem with
both Outlook Express and Windows Mail is that you can only access
your mail from the computer the program is installed on, unless you
set up a special Internet account as a go-between. Windows 7 offers
Windows Live Mail but you have to set it up, and their process is not
as simple as it is for other web mail programs. I don't suggest using

the email account provided by your Internet provider either, because you may change providers in the future. Instead, open a free account in Gmail (my favorite), Yahoo, MSN, etc. With web email such as Gmail, you can access your email from any computer or phone that has Internet access, and you don't have to worry about your computer dying and taking with it all your emails and contacts, since the program isn't stored on your hard drive.

Games

Start > All Programs > Accessories. FreeCell, Hearts, Internet Backgammon, Internet Checkers, Internet Hearts, Internet Reversi, Internet Spades, Minesweeper, Pin Ball, Solitaire, Spider Solitaire. You may have some or all of these or others I don't have. When you open the game, click on *Help* for instructions and rules.

Help

Can be accessed in different ways. Here are three of them:

(1) Click on the Start button and click on Help, OR

(2) Press the F1 key (upper left corner of your keyboard). Pressing F1 may bring up the entire Help program so that you can search for key words or click on a subject. Or pressing F1 may bring up related help topics according to what you were doing at the time that you pressed F1 (called context sensitive help), i.e., if you happen to be in a particular software, the Help menu that opens may be about that software, not about Windows. Or pressing F1 may bring up a small window that says "What do you want to do?" and you can type in a few words and press Enter, OR

(3) Open any folder and click on Help in the main menu.

If you're a beginner, explore the Help program. Depending on your Windows version, you can:

• Search for help on a specific topic.
• Troubleshoot a problem using the built-in troubleshooter.
• Complete a Windows tutorial.
• Read tips and techniques for using Windows.
• Find out what's new in your version of Windows.

Internet Explorer

Start or Start > All Programs > Internet Explorer. Internet Explorer is Microsoft's web browser. A web browser is a software program that interprets HyperText Markup Language (HTML) and other code that makes web pages display correctly. You can install other web browsers for free. See "Chapter 12 - The Internet."

NotePad

Start > All Programs > Accessories > NotePad. NotePad is a text editing software. It doesn't include formatting and it can't be used for really long documents, but you can use it for notes and to copy text from the Internet. It's also a good way to get rid of formatting that's been added to text so that you can paste the text into another program (such as an email) without the formatting. To use NotePad, right-click on your desktop, choose *New,* choose *text document.* Give the text document a name if you want to save it; if you're just using it to paste text into for copying back out again without the format, don't bother saving.

Paint

Start > All Programs > Accessories > Paint. Paint is a program used to draw, color, and edit pictures. If you don't have any pictures and you want to try it, take a screen shot of a folder on your desktop. Select the folder, press and hold down the *Alt* key and press the *Print Screen* key (this takes the screen shot). Open Paint and press Ctrl+V to paste the screen shot in. You can take a screen shot of your entire desktop by pressing the Print Screen button without the Alt key. There are lots of tutorials and videos on using Paint. Just search on the Internet for "How to use Microsoft Paint."

Snipping Tool (Vista, Windows 7)

Start > All Programs > Accessories > Snipping Tool. Snipping Tool is a screen shot program in Vista and Windows 7 which allows you to take a picture of anything on your desktop, including parts of web pages. Microsoft.com has a video showing how to use it. Just go there and search for *Snipping Tool* in the Search box.

System Restore

Start > All Programs > Accessories > System Tools > System Restore. System Restore is a system utility which allows you to restore your system settings to an earlier point in time. It's a lifesaver when your computer is suddenly not working correctly, because you can restore your system to a time when it *was* working correctly. You'll want to choose the most recent Restore point prior to having a problem with the computer. Windows should create Restore points for you automatically, but you should manually create a Restore point prior to installing new software, just in case something goes wrong with that installation.

This tool doesn't back up, restore, or affect your personal files (your documents, pictures, etc.) in any way. Open the program and take a look at it. For more detailed information, see your *Help* or search for "XP System Restore," "Windows 7 System Restore," etc.

Windows Defender and Windows Firewall

In XP and Vista, go to *Start > Control Panel > Security Center* to check settings for Defender and Firewall. In Windows 7, go to *Start > Control Panel* and you'll see the two programs in there.

Windows Defender is an anti-virus program that comes installed with Windows but it's very basic, so you should install another anti-virus program as soon as you can. A free one from Microsoft is called *Security Essentials*; you can download it from Microsoft.com. Other free programs include Avast and Avira. Download from the manufacturer website only and follow their installation instructions.

Windows Firewall protects your computer from intrusion on the Internet.

Your Notification Area will have icons for opening your anti-virus software. In Windows 7, the *Action Center* will tell you if your anti-virus software has stopped working or has any problems.

Windows Easy Transfer (Windows 7)

Start > All Programs > Accessories > System Tools > Windows Easy Transfer. Lets you copy files and settings (e.g., user accounts, documents, music, Internet favorites, videos, etc.) from one computer to another.

Windows Explorer

Start > All Programs > Accessories > Windows Explorer. Windows Explorer is a file manager application. It shows the hierarchical structure of your computer including external drives, network drives, etc. You can use Windows Explorer to browse through or search for anything on your computer and to copy, move, rename, and delete files and folders. See Chapter 11.

Windows Media Center (Windows 7, premium Vista)

Start > Windows Media Center OR *Start > All Programs > Windows Media Center.* Most versions of Windows 7 (and some versions of Vista) have Windows Media Center (WMC), which includes Windows Media Player (see next program) plus the ability to play and record live television and watch DVDs. WMC has an interface that allows you to run the program from your TV, if desired. When it comes to DVD media, check your PC manual to see what kind of DVD (DVD-R, -RW, +R, +RW, -RAM) your PC uses.

Windows Media Player

Start > Windows Media Player OR *Start > All Programs > Windows Media Player.* Windows Media Player (WMP) is the application that plays audio and video files. If you put a music CD into your CD/DVD drive—assuming you don't have a different player, such as iTunes set up as your default player—Windows Media Player should launch. WMP can also copy music *from* audio CDs (called "rip") or "burn" music or data from your computer *to* CDs.

Here's how I burned MP3 audio book files to a set of audio CDs in **Windows 7**:

1. I put a blank CD-R (Compact Disc-Recordable) into my DVD drive, and the AutoPlay menu in Fig. 9-4 opened.

Fig. 9-4. The Autoplay menu that opened when I inserted a
blank CD into the DVD drive in Windows 7.

2.   I clicked on "Burn an audio CD" and the window in Fig. 9-5
      opened. To burn *data* files rather than audio files, I'd choose
      "Burn files to disc," which uses Windows Explorer rather than
      Windows Media Player.

Fig. 9-5. The window that opened when I selected
"Burn an audio CD" as the action I wanted to take.

3.   I browsed to the folder of MP3 files which were numbered
      sequentially (001_Intro.mp3, Chapter01.mp3, Chapter02.
      mp3, etc.) and sorted in that order, selected all of the files, and

dragged them to the area that says "Drag items here."

4. Windows Media Player checked the files and gave me a "Burn list" showing the files that would fit on each CD (six CDs were needed) and I clicked "Start burn" (circled at the top of Fig. 9-6).

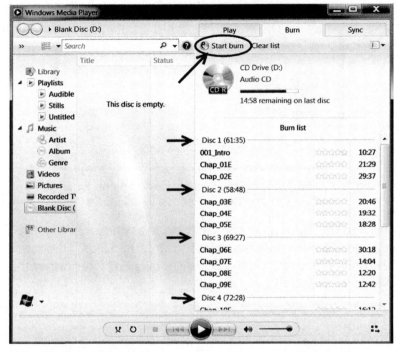

Fig. 9-6. WMP's assessment of the number of CDs required to burn the files I selected as a group.

5. As each CD was finished, Windows ejected the CD drawer and waited for me to replace the used CD with a new blank one. I could see the status on the left side of the window and also above the Burn List.

It was simple and fast. The only confusing part was when a CD finished and I put in a new one, the burn list moved up but the number of the Disc did not change. In other words, after Disc 1 was burned with the Intro, Chapter 1, and Chapter 2, the list of files under Disc 2 (Chapters 3, 4, and 5) moved up the list and were then listed under Disc 1.

In XP, the WMP interface isn't quite as smooth. First set your quality options by clicking Tools > Options > Copy Music tab > and slide the tab to *Best Quality* for audio files. When you put in a blank CD and the window opens, choose "Take no action." Then, in WMP, click the button on the left that says "Copy to CD." Click the Media Library button and find the songs to copy. Right-click on the songs and choose "Copy to Audio CD." If you choose more songs than will fit, Windows will show a message next to the songs that won't fit. Click the checkbox to remove the check for those songs. Next, click *Copy Music*, which is near the upper right corner.

If you have a portable music player, it should come with software that allows you to sync it to your PC, or else Windows should guide you through downloading the necessary software from online. Sometimes all you have to do is plug in your player and drag a song over. See "Removable Storage Devices" in Chapter 11.

Windows Movie Maker

Start > Windows Movie Maker OR *Start > All Programs > Windows Movie Maker.* With this program you can create home movies and slide shows from your photos and videos. Go to Microsoft.com and type "Windows movie maker" into the search box for more information.

WordPad

Start > All Programs > Accessories > WordPad. WordPad is a word processing software that includes formatting choices, i.e., you can change the appearance of the text with different fonts and styles, such as **Bold** and *Italics*, you can make bulleted lists, tab indents for paragraphs, etc. If you don't have Microsoft Word, use WordPad.

Installing Programs

Other Windows Programs

If you're looking for a program you thought came with Windows, look in these places:

(1) *Start > All Programs* OR
(2) *Start > All Programs > Accessories* OR
(3) *Start > All Programs > Accessories > System Tools*

If it's not there, try:

- in XP ... *Start > Control Panel > Add or Remove Programs* and scroll through the list
- in Windows 7 ... *Start > Control Panel > Programs and Features*

You can also search for it. (See Chapter 11 "Searching for a File" which also applies to programs and folders.)

If the program isn't listed, it may be available to install from your control panel. In Windows XP, in the *Add or Remove Programs* menu, click on *Add/Remove Windows Components*; in Windows 7, in the Control Panel's *Programs and Features* menu, click on *Turn Windows features on and off* (left side of menu). If the program is listed, click to add it. (You may be asked to insert your Windows CD if you purchased CDs.) If the program isn't in any of these places, it's not available to install.

Programs you purchase

When you purchase a program, it should install itself when you put in the CD/DVD or download the program from online, or else it should come with instructions for installing it.

Uninstalling a Program

If you install a program and then wish you hadn't, don't just delete the program folder. When installed, a program may change Windows systems files or may have its own set of system files that are not stored in the Program folder. So, to get rid of a program and the system changes that came with it, you must *uninstall* it.

In XP go to *Start > Control Panel > Add or Remove Programs;* in Windows 7 go to *Start > Control Panel > Programs and Features.* Scroll through the list of programs, click on the one you want to remove, and click the *Uninstall* or *Remove* button.

10 - Folders

The folders of Windows XP, Vista, and 7 display, for the most part, the same information; you just have to get there in slightly different ways. Windows XP and Windows 7 folders are shown in Figs. 10-1 and 10-3, respectively. Vista folders are almost identical to Windows 7. It doesn't matter which version of Microsoft Windows you use as long as you're willing to find your way around.

Windows XP Folder Parts

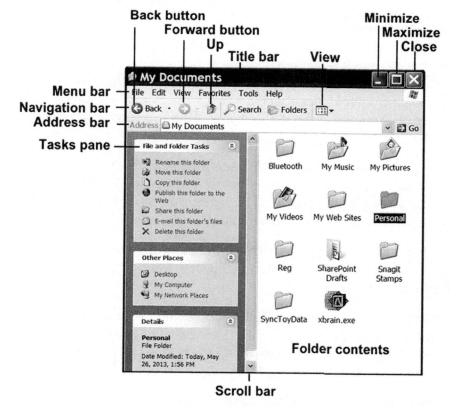

Fig. 10-1. The parts of a Windows XP folder (icon view).

Starting from the top and working down ...

Title bar - Tells the name of the folder or file. The title bar and its items are covered in Chapter 7.

Menu bar - Shows the menu headings *File, Edit, View, Favorites, Tools, and Help*. The options that appear on the drop-down menu for each of these headings changes depending on the item you select.

- **File** - This menu gives you the same options you get by right-clicking on the item.
- **Edit** - *Undo, Redo, Select All, Cut, Copy, Paste* are on this menu (you can use keyboard shortcuts for these instead). Others are *Copy to Folder* or *Move to Folder*, and then you would browse to a folder.
- **View** - Lets you choose which toolbars to show or hide, the view of the folder, and the columns to display. Almost all the choices can be found elsewhere in the folder, so unless you are making several changes at one time, you probably won't use the View menu to make them.
- **Favorites** - Shows your Internet Explorer favorite websites and lets you add, delete, etc.
- **Tools** - Folder options are on this menu. See "Changing Folder Options" later in this chapter.
- **Help** - You can find out about your Windows version here or access the *Help* program.

Navigation bar - Contains the ***Back button*** (arrow pointing left) which takes you back to the last folder you visited. Click the arrow pointing to the right to return. The ***Up button*** takes you up one hierarchal level in your file or folder path (see Chapter 11).

On the right side of this bar, the ***Folders button*** lets you toggle between viewing the **Task Pane** (shown in Fig. 10-1) and the **Folders Pane** (shown in Fig. 10-2).

Address bar - This shows the location of the folder within your computer. The folder I clicked on (Personal) in Fig. 10-1 is located in *My Documents* folder. I can make the full file path show in the Address bar (see "Changing Folder Options" below).

Task Pane - Shows available ***tasks*** for the item you select, as well as ***details*** of the item, and ***other places*** you can navigate to. If the Task Pane isn't showing in your XP folder, click on *Tools* on the Menu bar, then *Folder Options*. Under the *General* tab, the first item will be *Tasks*. Click in the button next to "Show common tasks in folders."

Folder contents - Shows the contents of the folder, displayed according to the *View* you've chosen. In Figs. 10-1 and 10-2, the contents show in *Icon* view. Fig. 10-3 displays in *Details* view.

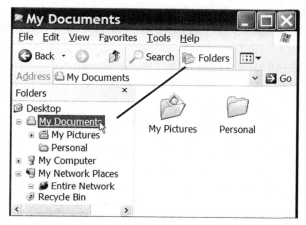

Fig. 10-2. Clicking on the Folders button of an XP folder replaces the Task Pane with the Folders Pane shown above. Click on it again to return to the Task Pane view shown in Fig. 10-1.

Windows 7 (and Vista) Folder Parts

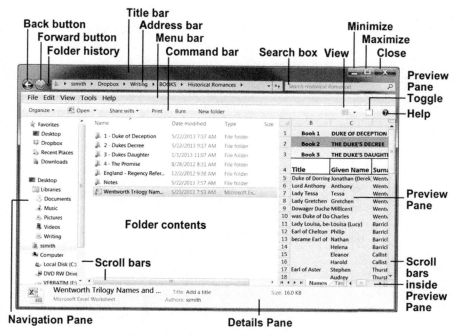

Fig. 10-3. The parts of a Windows 7 folder in Details view.

Again, from the top down, then across …

Title bar - Same as XP. Tells the name of the folder or file.

Address bar - Shows the address (location) of the folder within the computer. Other items on the Address bar are: the ***folder history*** drop-down menu button, which is the small triangle pointing down, located to the left of the address; the ***navigational buttons*** (same as XP), and the **Search box**. To search, type a word or phrase into this box and click the magnifying glass, and Windows will search the folder for any sub-folder or file containing those words.

Menu bar - See description for XP items above. In Windows 7 menu headings are the same as XP, except no *Favorites*. Show or hide the Menu bar by clicking on *Organize > Layout > Menu bar.*

Command bar - In Vista and Windows 7, depending on the item you've clicked on and the folder you're in, the possible tasks on the Command bar change. ***Organize*** should always show (see Fig. 10-4). Everything else on the Command bar is a task to apply to the item you've selected. Click on various options to see what happens, then click *Cancel.*

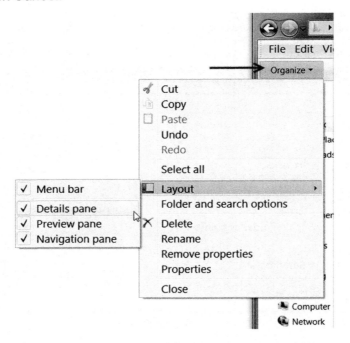

Fig. 10-4. The Organize menu in a Windows 7 folder.

Click on *Organize*, click on *Layout*, and you can choose to show any or all of these four parts of a Windows 7 folder: *Menu bar, Details Pane, Preview Pane, Navigation Pane.*

To the far right of the Command bar are three more items: the *View icon*, the *Preview Pane toggle*, and a *Help icon*.

Navigation Pane - This is the same as the Folders Pane in XP. Windows 7's Navigation Pane includes *Favorites*, which are the places you frequent; *Libraries*, which are groups of folders (see Chapter 11); *Homegroup*, which shows PCs that are grouped together by a network (for example, your personal laptop, your spouse's computer, and your children's PC, if you grouped them together in order to share files); *Computer*, which shows your drives and is handy if you plug in a flash drive (also called memory stick or thumb drive); and *Networks*. You can change the Navigation folder view through the Folder Options menu. See "Changing Folder Options" below.

Folder contents - Same as XP. Shows the contents of the folder, displayed according to the chosen *View*. In Figs. 10-1 and 10-2, the contents show in *Icon* view. Fig. 10-3 displays in *Details* view.

Details Pane - Shows details about the selected item.

Preview Pane - Click on a file listed in the folder, and you can see a preview of it. In Fig. 10-3 I've clicked on an Excel spreadsheet, so that's what I can preview. Only files (not folders) can be previewed. Click on the *Preview Pane toggle* to the right of the Command bar to hide or show the *Preview Pane*.

Changing the View

You can view a folder's content as icons, a list, extra large icons (also called thumbnails), etc. The quickest way to change your view is to click on the View icon on the Navigation bar (XP) or Command bar (Vista, Windows 7). Fig. 10-5 shows the various choices.

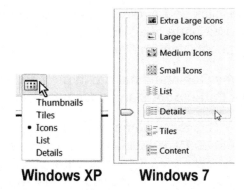

Windows XP   Windows 7

Fig. 10-5. Options for viewing folders in Windows XP and Windows 7.

The above choices are also available from the View menu. Don't get the *View* menu (part of the File, Edit, **View**, Tools, Help menu bar) confused with the View *tab* which is on the *Tools > Folder Options* menu. The **View menu** is covered here, and you should select those settings first. The View *tab* on the *Tools > Folder Options* menu is covered in the next section, "Changing Folder Options." You should select View tab settings *after* the View menu settings because the View tab allows you to apply all the settings made under both menus to every folder as a default view.

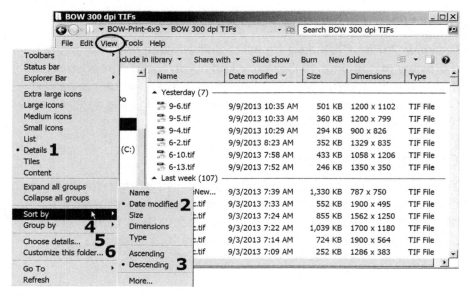

Fig. 10-6. A folder's View menu in Windows 7. This folder is in Details view, grouped and sorted by Date modified in descending date order.

In the View menu you can set a default view for your folders. My default view is the **Details view** (item number 1 in Fig. 10-6) because I like to sort by **Date modified** (item 2) - **Descending date** (item 3) to see the files I most recently worked on at the top of the folder. I also like to **group them by Date modified** (click on item 4, "Group by" to select grouping) as well. But you can choose any view for your default view.

After choosing the default view, sort, and grouping, click on **"Choose details ..."** (item 5) and a menu similar to the one in Fig. 10-7 will open. Here you decide which items to display as columns in a Details or List view and the width of each column. You can also decide on the order of the columns, or you can do that manually by closing this menu and dragging the columns around by their titles.

If you choose a Thumbnail or Icon view, instead of List or Details, the details will show in the Details pane when you click on an item (there aren't any columns when items are displayed as icons or thumbnails).

Under the View menu you can also choose **Customize this folder** (item 6 in Fig. 10-6) to change the properties of the selected folder. Choices include the folder picture or icon that's displayed.

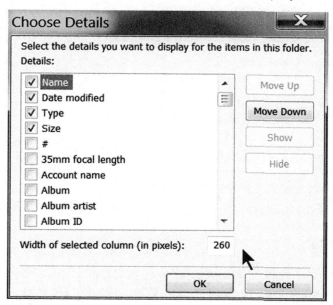

Fig. 10-7 A folder's *View > Choose Details* menu in Windows 7 where you can select the columns/details to show about the folder's content.

Once you have a default view, go to **Tools > Folder Options > View tab** and click to apply this folder view to all folders (see next section).

Changing Folder Options

In any folder in XP, Vista, or 7, click on *Tools > Folder Options*. In Vista and Windows 7 you can also get to the Folder Options menu from *Organize > Folder and Search Options > Folder Options*.

The Windows 7 menu has three tabs: General, View, and Search. The XP menu (Fig. 10-8) has General, View, File Types, Offline Files. *General* and *View* are discussed below. The *Search* tab allows you to set options for the Search indexing and options. *File Types* tab lets you change the programs that Windows uses to open a particular kind of file. See Chapter 11 for more on files.

Fig. 10-8. Folder Options menu showing choices under General tab in XP.

General tab

- **Tasks** - XP only. Choose to show the folder's Task Pane (shown on the left in Fig. 10-1) or to use Windows classic folder view.
- **Browse folders** - All versions. You can have every folder open in the same window, which means each time you open a folder,

the one you're in at that time disappears and the new one takes its place, OR you can open each folder in its own window, which means both folders remain open.

- **Click items as follows** - You can choose for your mouse to open items with a single click or a double click.
- **Navigation pane** - Vista and Windows 7 only. Checking the box next to "Show all folders" gives an expanded hierarchal list in the Navigation Pane. See Fig. 10-9.

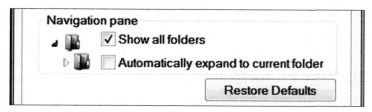

Fig. 10-9. *Tools > Folder Options > General tab > Navigation pane* settings (Windows 7)

View tab

On *Tools > Folder Options > View* tab there are two areas: *Folder views* and *Advanced settings*.

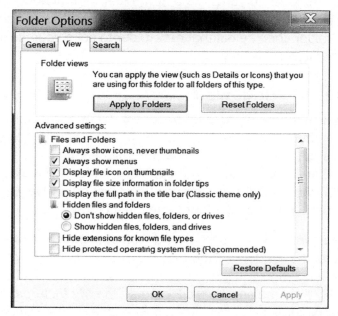

Fig. 10-10. Folder Options View tab in Windows 7.

Under *Folder views*, there's an option to **Apply to Folders**. Do this if the view of your current folder is set up the way you'd like all folders to be set up as a starting point. You can then change folders individually. If you change a folder to, for example, Thumbnail view, Windows 7 will remember to display that folder in Thumbnail view, though it displays all others in the default view.

Under **Advanced settings**, the items I've checked in Fig. 10-10 are ones I always select. There are more options you can scroll to see. One of those is "Show pop-up descriptions for folder and desktop items." Check the boxes for the ones you think you want. You can change your selection any time.

Making New Folders

Right-click where you want to create a folder (desktop, inside another folder, etc.) and choose *New > Folder.* The folder name should be highlighted when the folder appears. Type the name you want the folder to have.

You can also make new folders "on the fly" while performing other tasks. If, for instance, you're saving a file and you browse to the folder and then realize you'd like a new folder for that document, you can click in the folder contents area or on the desktop and create your new folder, then select that new folder to save your file in. (You can rename items this way too.)

Libraries in Windows 7

Libraries are a new feature in Windows 7. Windows starts you off with four of them: Documents, Pictures, Movies, and Videos, with two folders in each category: *your* folder for that category and the *Public* folder for that category. So, if you open any folder and look at your Navigation Pane, you'll see *Libraries* listed just below Desktop, and the four above-mentioned folders listed just below that.

Click on *Pictures* under *Libraries* and look at the folder contents. At the top of the window will be *Pictures Library* and below that "Includes: 2 locations." If you hover over that, the two locations will show as *My Pictures* and *Public Pictures.* The *My Pictures* library will show your pictures that aren't shared with others. The *Public Pictures* folder will show pictures that other users (or you) have placed there plus shared system pictures such as desktop background images.

The Libraries feature is handy if you have different folders you want to access from one location. For instance, if you're working on three different projects, you can add those three folders to one library so you can quickly switch between the folders when working. The folders will remain stored in their original places but will be available to you from that library. You can set up a library either from the folders you want to include or from the library.

The first way is to create a library from the folder you want in there:

1. **Browse to the folder you want to include in a new library**. You can browse using the Navigation Pane or not; your choice.
2. Select the folder (*House Repairs* is selected in Fig. 10-11) and **click "Include in Library" on the Command bar** .
3. When the menu pops up, you can choose an existing library or click *Create new library* and give the library a name.
4. Repeat steps 1 and 2 for the other folders you want in this library. If you created a new library, select it in step 3.

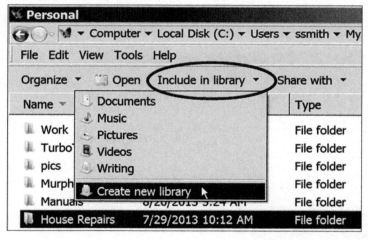

Fig. 10-11. Creating a new library from the folder that will go in the library.

The second way is to create the library first, then put folders in it (turn on your folder's navigation pane for this one):

1. **Click on *Libraries* in the Navigation Pane** of any folder.
2. In the folder contents window, **right-click and choose *New > Library*** from the menu (see Fig. 10-12).
3. Name it whatever you want.
4. Click on your new library in the folder's Navigation Pane and

click on the ***Include a folder*** button in the window. In Fig. 10-13, my new library is called "Work To Do."

5.   Browse to find and select folders to add to your new library.

Fig. 10-12. Creating a new library by browsing to Libraries in the Navigation Pane first. A new library created this way is empty until you add the folders.

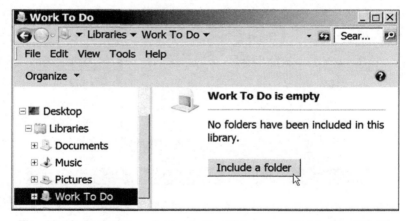

Fig. 10-13. Including a folder in the library created in Fig. 10-12.

You can remove folders from a library without deleting the actual folders on your computer. So, once I've finished a project, I can remove that folder from my *Work To Do* library by right-clicking on the folder in the Navigation pane and choosing "Remove location from library." Now when I get on my PC, I can go straight to this *Work To Do* library, and all my projects are available from this location.

11 - Files

What is a file?

A file is a collection of information stored in electronic format. A file can be a photo, video, spreadsheet, letter, program file, etc. All files have a name, given to them by their creator at the time the file is saved for the first time. This file name consists of the actual name followed by a period (called dot) and a 3 or 4-letter extension. The extension tells Windows what type of file it is so that Windows will use the correct application to open the file. Note: your PC may be set up so that you can't see the extensions but you can change that in your *Folder Options* > *View* tab by unchecking the box that says "Hide extensions for known file types."

Files used by a software program are named by the software programmer. Files *you* create, such as letters or other documents, are named by you. In some cases, files are named automatically, such as with a camera's digital photo files which will have a generic name (picture1.jpg, picture2.jpg, etc.) and you can rename them individually or in batches.

A program may open only one specific file type or it may open several. Also, more than one program may be able to open the same type of file. In that case, you make the choice, depending on the software you like to use. For example, Microsoft Word will save its files with the .docx extension by default for versions of Word 2007 and later, but you can choose to save that file with .htm to open it using Internet Explorer or another web browser.

The only files you should rename, move around, or delete are the files *you* create. Leave the other files alone. Deleting a file you didn't create may cause your PC to quit working.

Here are some common file extensions:

- css - cascading style sheet, used to display website styles
- doc, docx - Microsoft Word document
- dot, dotx - Microsoft Word document template

- epub - electronic book (ebook) file that can be opened by electronic reading devices and web browsers
- exe - executable file that opens an application
- htm, html - hypertext markup language file, used to display websites
- jpg, jpeg, png, gif, tif, tiff, wmf - image files
- pdf - Adobe portable document file which can be opened in Adobe Reader, Adobe Acrobat, or by web browsers
- ppt, pptx - Microsoft PowerPoint presentation file
- txt - text file
- xls, xlsx - Microsoft Excel file
- zip - a format which allows you to compress one or more files together as one file for archiving or distribution purposes

Selecting a default program to open a file type

If you have more than one program that can open the same type of file, Windows will choose one as the default program for opening those files. To open with a different program, you can right-click on the file, click on "Open with" and select the program you want. That's good for occasional use. If you want a different program to open that type of file all the time, here's how you change that.

- In XP, open any folder, click *Tools* > *Folder Options* > *File Types.*
- In Vista and Windows 7, go to *Start* > *Default Programs* OR *Start* > *Control Panel* > *Default Programs*; click on "Associate a file type with a program."

A window will open and load all your computer's known file types. Find the file extension that's opening in the wrong program. Click on *Change* and select the program you want to open that file type with.

What is a file path?

The file path shows the file's location in relation to the computer. Windows uses the file path to find, open, save, or delete a file. Paths never start with the file itself; the file is always at the end of the path. The beginning of the path is the highest level of storage and each sub-level of storage is included in the path. As a simple comparison, if I displayed the path of a screwdriver in your house, it might be:

- *house\garage\tool cart\top drawer\screwdriver*

The path of a screwdriver at *my* house might be:

- *house\kitchen\junk drawer\screwdriver OR*
- *house\garage\pegboard\peg\screwdriver OR*
- *house\garage\tool cabinet\second drawer\screwdriver*

The reason I might have several different paths to the same item is because I keep coming up with a better place to store something—or so I think. But the truth is that I just end up with several places where I've stored the same item at different times, and inevitably, I forget which place I decided was best. The result is that when I'm looking for the item, I can't find it. It's a very bad habit which I urge you not to get into with your PC files.

Hard Drive and Letter Designations: C Drive, D Drive, etc.

Back in the olden days, the A and B drives were for floppy disks, which hold about 2 MB and therefore aren't used much now. If a computer had a built-in (hard) drive, it was called the C drive. This naming convention continues today. Some PCs have more than one hard drive; sometimes a second one is added because the first one is full, or the owner partitioned the hard drive in order to have two drives. In those cases, the second hard drive may be called the D drive. The letters for the hard drives are permanently designated to those drives. If you have a built-in CD or DVD drive, it probably also has a letter permanently associated with it. Maybe it's the D drive or the E drive.

Letter designations for *removable* storage devices will change depending on the order in which the drives are plugged in. If you plug an external flash drive into your USB port, Windows may assign the letter F to it. If you leave that drive plugged in and then plug your camera into another port, the camera drive may be assigned the letter G. If you remove both the flash drive and the camera and then plug in only the camera, the camera drive will be assigned the letter F (instead of G) since F will be the next letter available.

Fig. 11-1. USB connector on left; on right are two USB ports on a notebook computer. Most devices (printer, mouse, keyboard, removable storage device such as a camera or flash drive) connect to a computer this way.

Transferring Files to and from Removable Storage Devices

You can copy files to many types of removable media:

- CDs hold 650 to 700 Megabytes (MB) of information.
- DVDs generally hold 4.7 gigabytes (GB) (there are a little over 1,000 MB in one GB).
- Flash drives—including those in a camera, MP3 player, etc.—and external hard drives vary greatly, holding anywhere from a few hundred MB to several hundred GB.

Copying data files to a flash drive

1. Plug your flash drive or other removable disk into your PC. Most plug into a USB port (see Fig. 11-1) and the connector can only go into the port one way. Don't force the plug if it doesn't seem to work. Just flip it over and try again. Once it's connected, the AutoPlay menu in Fig. 11-2 will open.
2. To copy files to the removable drive, choose "Open folder to view files" and the drive's folder will open on your desktop.
3. Assuming the folder with the files to be copied is already open on your desktop, drag the folders or files into the drive's folder. Windows will copy (not move) the files. You can also copy the files using Windows Explorer (see the section "Windows Explorer" near the end of this chapter).

Fig. 11-2. The AutoPlay menu that appears when you plug a
flash drive or other type of removable disk into your PC.

When you finish copying files to the flash drive, don't pull the drive
out or you may corrupt data. XP, Vista, and Windows 7 all require
that you disconnect a drive or other media by first requesting permission. To remove a connected drive, right-click on the "Safely remove
hardware" icon (circled in Fig. 11-3) in your Notification area on the
taskbar. Select the device to disconnect. You can also open My
Computer, right-click on the drive for that device, and choose *Eject*.

Fig. 11-3. The icon you right-click on to remove an external storage
device or other media hooked up to your computer.

You can also transfer data files to a CD.

Copying data files to a CD in Windows XP

1. Put a blank CD into your CD drive, and when the Autoplay
    menu opens, choose "Open writable CD folder using Windows
    Explorer" and click OK. The folder inside the CD Drive will open
    with an empty area for you to drag your files into.

2. Go to the folder where the folders or files that you want to copy are located and drag them over to the CD drive folder.
3. When you're finished dragging, click "Write these files to CD" in the *CD Writing* Tasks pane on the left. Name the CD (16 or fewer characters), click *Next*, and wait for *Finish*.

Copying data files to a CD in Vista or Windows 7

1. Put in the blank CD and the AutoPlay menu will open. Choose "Burn files to disc."
2. Name the disc and choose the way you want the files burned.
3. Drag the files over and let Windows do the rest.

Another way to copy to a CD **in Windows 7** is to select the folder or files you want to burn to CD and click *Burn* in the folder's Command bar. Windows will tell you to insert a blank CD, etc.

Searching for a File

Here are several ways to locate a file. Try them all:

(1) Via Recent Documents/Items on the Start menu.

For a file you recently worked on, try this first.

1. Click on the Start button.
2. Click on or mouse over *My Recent Documents/Recent Items*.
3. Click on the file's name and the file will open. At this point you don't need to do anything else if all you want is to find the file so you can work on it.

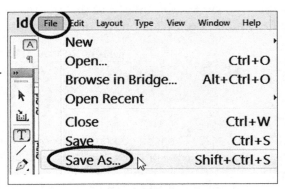

Fig. 11-4. The *File > Save As* menu choice for this InDesign book.

4. However, if you want to know exactly where this file is being stored, click on *File > Save As* (see Fig. 11-4.)
5. When the *Save As* window opens (Fig. 11-5), you can see where the file currently resides on your computer, but you can't tell

where that folder resides in relation to the rest of the computer. To see the complete file path, click on the drop-down menu where it says "Save in" at the top of the window.

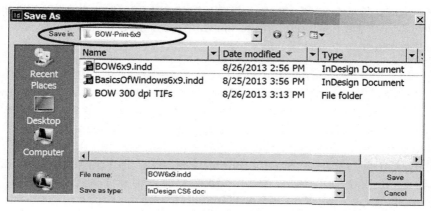

Fig. 11-5. The *Save As* window that opens for this book in Windows 7 shows that this file is saved in a folder called "BOW-Print-6x9" (circled).

When I click on the drop-down menu arrow (circled in Fig. 11-6) to the right of the "BOW-Print-6x9" folder name, a drop-down menu opens, showing the BOW-Print-6x9 folder's location in relation to the rest of my computer. In this particular case, from looking at the hierarchy displayed, I see that the file is located at *ssmith\Dropbox\ Writing\BOOKS\BasicsOfWindows\BOW-Print-6x9* (inside the rectangle). The name of the file, BOW6x9.indd, is displayed in the white File Name box near the bottom of the window.

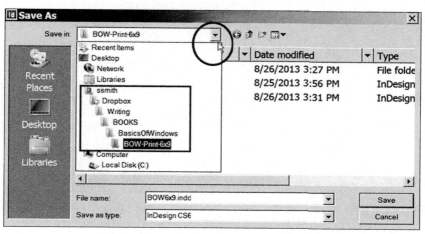

Fig. 11-6. Clicking on the drop-down menu of the *Save As* window in Windows 7 in order to see the file path.

The complete file path would begin with C:\Users, which doesn't show in this figure. *C*, the hard drive, is the highest level of storage. *Users* is the next level because Windows separates everything according to the user name. *ssmith* (my user name) is the next level. *Dropbox* is the next level in the file path, and so on, all the way down to the folder called *BOW-Print-6x9*.

To save this file somewhere else I can click on any of the folders in that hierarchy list and click the **Save** button. However, I will then have two copies of the same file, which can cause problems if I continue editing the file. Note that Windows doesn't care if I have a bunch of files with the same name. As long as the files are stored in different places, they will each have a different file path. But believe me when say it's not a good idea. I may update a file one day and then accidentally open one of the other files with the same name and update it the next day. To keep both files, I should rename the older one to include the date or add "previous" or "old" to the name.

Another way to locate a file is:

(2) Via Recent Items on the taskbar (Windows 7 only)

In Windows 7, right-click on a program's icon on the taskbar to see recent items or past history (called a "jump list") for that program. In Fig. 11-7 I right-clicked on the Microsoft Word icon on the taskbar.

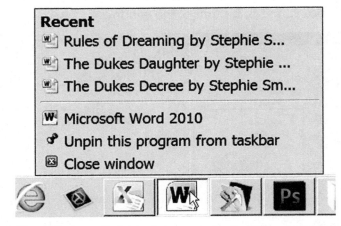

Fig. 11-7. The Windows 7 right-click menu for the Microsoft Word icon on my taskbar, showing my most recently opened documents, the Microsoft Word program, and an option to unpin the program from the taskbar. To open one of the recent documents, just click on it.

(3) Via Recent documents inside the software program.

As in the first two examples, this is another "recent" item lookup, so it only works for files recently worked on.

1. Open the application you created the file in.

2. Once the application is open, click on the File menu and look for a choice that includes the word "recent." Click on that for a list of files you recently opened (see Fig. 11-8).

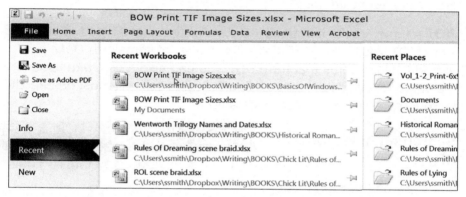

Fig. 11-8. In Microsoft Excel I clicked on *Files* on the menu and selected *Recent*. The left column of the folder contents shows me recent files (workbooks) and the right column shows recent places (folders) I've been.

(4) Using the Search program.

The Windows 7 search is much improved over earlier versions. Before I give you specifics, I'll give you some general information.

General search criteria

Search criteria is not case sensitive. *Duke* or *duke* will return the same results.

Putting words in quotation marks returns items with the exact string of words. Ex: *"Duke of Deception"* returns items that contain that exact phrase, whereas typing *Duke of Deception* without quotes returns items with those three words anywhere, in any order.

AND returns results containing all search criteria. Ex: Results for *Duke AND doc* will contain both these terms—mostly Word documents (.doc or .docx file extensions) with the word *Duke* in the file, title, or properties, but this InDesign file I'm typing in right now will also show up in those results because both terms are written in it. You can also type **Duke + doc.** If I searched for **Duke doc** I would most likely get the same results because AND is implied, but occasionally, with some search engines, putting in the AND or the + makes a difference.

OR returns results containing any of the search criteria. Ex: **Duke OR doc** returns a much larger set of results, i.e., every item with *Duke* and every item with *doc*.

NOT returns results that don't include the item that's typed after the word NOT. Ex: **Duke NOT doc** returns a list of items with *Duke* but excludes Duke items that have *doc*. You can also type **Duke -doc** for the same results. Note: when using the minus sign, it must be directly in front of the word with no space after it.

Searching in Windows XP

1. Click on the Start menu.
2. Click on *Search*.
3. The Search menu opens with choices similar to Fig. 11-9.
4. If you select *Pictures, music, or video*, the menu in Fig. 11-10 opens.
5. Check the appropriate boxes, type into the fields with any information you have, or click on advanced options.
6. When you've entered all your criteria, click *Search* to see your search results. The location of the stored files will show under the "Folder" column.

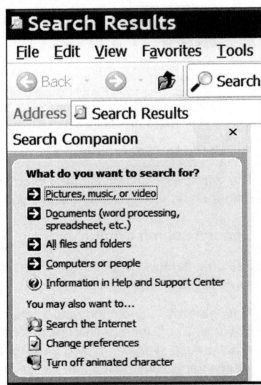

Fig. 11-9. Search Results window in XP. Choose first from the items on the left and another window will open to offer more search criteria.

The more info you put in, the less time it takes Windows to search. If the file doesn't show up in the results, you may want to remove one of the search criterion so as to broaden the search.

Searching in Windows 7

In Windows 7 you can search from the Search field at the bottom of the Start menu or from the Search field in the upper right corner of any folder.

Whichever box you search from, as you type the search words into the box, Windows will begin displaying a list of matches for you. As you add letters to the search string, Windows filters the results.

You can use various search filters in Windows 7 also:

Fig. 11-10. Additional Search Criteria for Pictures, music, or video in XP.

- **Modified:***07/13/2013* returns items modified on July 13, 2013 only.

- **Modified:***2012* returns items modified during calendar year 2012.

- **System.Kind:***<>picture* returns items are aren't pictures. <> means "is not."

You can go to the Windows 7 website and search for "How to search in Windows 7" to learn more: *http://windows.microsoft.com/en-us/ windows7/products/features/windows-search*

If you search from the Start menu, Windows will search across the indexed items in your entire computer starting with the folders Windows set up for your files, e.g., Documents, Pictures, Videos, etc. (This is one of the reasons I suggested you use the folders Windows sets up for you to save time.) Results will be sorted into groups such as Documents, Music, etc. Only the top few choices are listed but you can click on any of the section headings displayed and a window will open to show all of them. To see where a file is stored, right-click on the file and choose "Open file location" (which will open the folder the file is stored in) OR click "See more results" (which will open a Search results folder where the Address bar will show the location of the selected item).

If you search from a folder window, Windows will search for items in that folder. To broaden a search to include more folders, click on a higher folder level in the Navigation Pane. The Search box displays the name of the folder that will be searched. See Fig. 11-11.

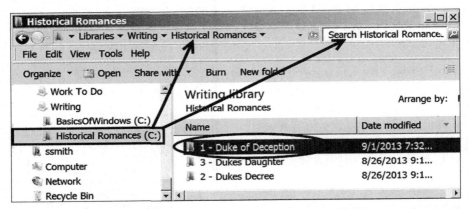

Fig. 11-11. When searching from a Windows 7 folder, Windows searches the folder selected in the Navigation Pane.

In Fig. 11-11, even though I've clicked on the folder called *1 - Duke of Deception* (circled) in the folder content area on the right, the Search box at the top right (with the magnifying glass) shows that the *Historical Romances* folder will be searched because it's selected (in the rectangle) in the navigation pane. To search only in the *1 - Duke of Deception* folder, I'd expand the Historical Romances folder in the navigation pane and select the *1 - Duke of Deception* folder. The Search box would then change to "Search 1 - Duke of Deception." **Windows searches the folder selected in the navigation pane.**

Windows Explorer

I covered copying and moving folders and files in Chapter 3 using cut/copy and paste and also drag and drop. Here's the way to copy, move, or delete folders and files using *Windows Explorer.*

Copying and Moving

1.   In XP, open any folder. If the Task Pane shows on the left of the folder, click on the *Folders* icon in the Navigation bar of the folder (under the Menu bar).

   In Windows 7 or Vista, make sure the Navigation Pane is open (click on *Organize > Layout* and make sure there's a checkmark next to Navigation Pane).

2.   Browse through the folder hierarchy to find the folder you want to copy/move. In XP, click on the + sign to show subfolders within folders. In Windows 7 and Vista, click the triangle to the left of the folder name.

   In both cases the subfolders will be slightly indented below the main folder. Files will show on the right once you've clicked on the lowest level of folder in the navigation pane. In Fig. 11-12 I clicked on *Scotland*, the only folder under *Scotland and Castles*. Now the files I want to move show in the folder content area.

3.   Make sure the location folder you plan to copy or move the items *to* is also showing in the folders on the left. (Close up any high level folders you don't need to look inside so they aren't showing in the Navigation/Folders list.)

4.   Go to the folder or files you want to move/copy, select them, and then either:
   • Drag it/them to the new location; OR
   • Rght-click and select *Copy*, then go to the new location and right-click and select *Paste*, OR
   • Use one of the other methods to move/copy and paste, such as keyboard shortcuts; OR
   • Alternatively, you can select those files, click on *Edit > Copy to folder* or *Move to folder* (on the folder menu bar) and then browse to select the folder to move the items to.

If you make a mistake, press Ctrl+Z or click (on the folder menu) on *Edit > Undo*.

In Fig. 11-12, I moved the file called "Castles in the Middle Ages.doc" from the *Scotland folder* to the *Medieval References* folder.

1. I clicked on the triangle next to the folder called *England - Refer-ences* so that its subfolder, *Medieval References* (the folder I want to move my file *to*), could be seen in the navigation pane.
2. I clicked on the triangle next to the folder called *Scotland and Castles* so that its subfolder, *Scotland*, opened, revealing its files (including the Word document I want to move) in the folder content area.
3. I dragged the Word document to the *Medieval References* folder and dropped it in.

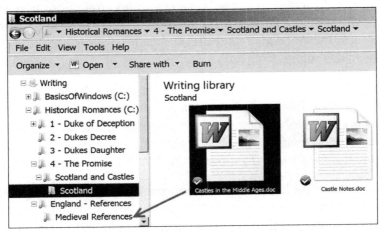

Fig. 11-12. Using Windows Explorer to move a file from one folder (Scotland) to another (Medieval References).

Navigating between folders

Both Figs. 11-12 and 11-13 have the same *Scotland* folder open showing the same two Word files in the folder content area. You can tell that the folder *Scotland* is the open folder because it's the last folder showing in the Address bar of each picture. You can also tell by looking at the Windows Explorer folders view (navigation pane) on the left in Fig. 11-12 because the folder *Scotland* is selected.

Fig. 11-13. Navigating between folders by clicking in the Address bar (Windows 7 only).

To navigate to a different folder in this hierarchy you can use the Windows Explorer navigation pane as described above, but you can also use the Address bar. In Fig. 11-13, I clicked in the Address bar on the triangle directly to the right of the Historical Romances folder. A drop-down menu opened showing the subfolders inside the Historical Romances folder. I could click on one of those folders, or I could click on the Historical Romances folder which is highlighted in the Address bar to open that folder instead. Clicking on the triangles between folders in the Address bar is another way to see the subfolders, similar to expanding the folders in the navigation pane.

Renaming Folders and Files

There are a couple of ways to rename a folder or file. You should not, however, rename programs. If you make a shortcut to the program and want to rename the shortcut, fine. But leave the actual programs alone.

Renaming a single folder or file

(1) **Select the item and press the F2 key** on your keyboard. The name should become selected. Then type the new name. The previous name will disappear with your first keystroke as long as the name is selected (Note: If the extension should happen to become selected along with the name, do not change it), OR

(2) **Right-click on the folder or file, and select Rename** from the pop-up menu. The name should become selected. Type the new name as mentioned above, OR

(3) **Click once to select the item. Wait a moment and then click again**, this time inside the name. The name should become selected so that you can type a new name. If you click a third time inside the name, you'll get a cursor and can add or delete letters without replacing the entire name.

Renaming several files at one time

If you don't care about the order of the files you rename, you don't need to sort first.

1. **Select the files** by using either the shift key (to select the first and last file and all files in between) or the ctrl key (to select files individually that are not together).

2. **Press the F2 key.**
3. **Type the new name and press ENTER.** Windows will name all the files with the name you typed and a numbering sequence beginning with (1). See Fig. 11-14 where I selected seven photos to rename.

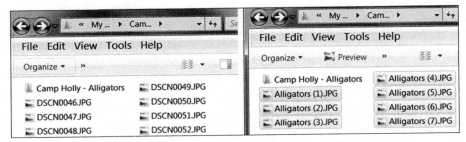

Fig. 11-14. I selected all the picture files in the folder on the left, pressed F2, and typed Alligators. Windows renamed the photos Alligators (1) through Alligators (7).

If the order of the file numbering *does* matter to you, then before renaming, change the folder to *Details* view and sort using the desired column(s) until the file order is the way you want. Windows will number the files starting from the top of the list.

Creating Shortcuts to Programs, Folders, or Files

A shortcut is an icon that represents a file, folder, or application stored on your hard drive. You can place a shortcut in any convenient location, but the actual item (called target item) stays in its saved location. You can open the target item from the shortcut. Anything else you do with the shortcut, such as rename, delete, or move, affects the shortcut itself and not the target item.

You can usually tell whether an icon represents a shortcut or the target item by the small curved arrow (or lack thereof). If you're not sure, right-click on the item and select *Properties* to find out.

Fig. 11-15. Icons on the left with arrows are shortcuts. The two icons on the right are not.

Deleting a shortcut won't delete the target item, and vice-versa. If you delete a target item **in XP** and then try to open it using the shortcut, you'll get a message that the item can't be found. The same thing *may* happen if you move either the target item or the shortcut after the shortcut is made because Windows XP will look for those items in their original locations. XP will give you the chance to browse for the target item and reconnect it to the shortcut, but it's usually easier to cancel, delete the shortcut, and create another one.

Unlike XP, **Windows 7** knows if you deleted the target item and will tell you. Also unlike XP, Windows 7 will keep your shortcut attached to the target, even if you move the target item or the shortcut around.

Here are several ways to create a shortcut; try them all. First close any unneeded windows and make sure an area of your desktop is showing. To make a shortcut to a folder or file see options (1) - (4). To make a shortcut to a program, see options (5) - (9).

(1) Right-click on the item, choose the appropriate option.

Right-click on the item, and release the mouse button. A menu of options will pop up. You can either:
- Click on *Create Shortcut* and the shortcut will be created there. You can then drag it to another location, OR
- Click on *Send to* and choose *Desktop (Create Shortcut)* to put the shortcut on your desktop (see Fig. 11-16).

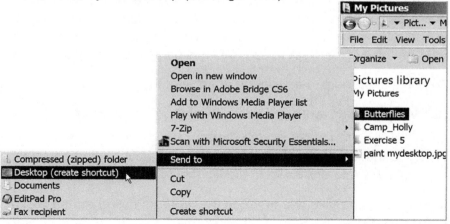

Fig. 11-16. Creating a shortcut to a folder by right-clicking on the folder (called Butterflies on the right) and choosing *Send to* > (in the middle menu) and selecting *Desktop (create shortcut)* in the final menu (on the left).

(2) Right-click on the item, Drag and Drop.

1. Right-click on the item and hold the button down.
2. Drag the item to the desktop (or wherever you want to put the shortcut) and drop the item there.
3. Choose *Create shortcut here* from the menu that pops up. The target item will remain where it was and a shortcut to it will appear on the desktop.

(3) Select the item, choose *Create Shortcut* from the folder's File menu.

1. Select the item.
2. Click on the *File* menu of the folder, and choose *Create Shortcut*. The shortcut will be created there, and you can drag it to another location.

(4) Right-click on desktop, choose *New*, choose *Shortcut*.

1. Right-click on your desktop, choose *New*, select *Shortcut*.
2. Browse to the item, click on it, and click *OK*. The browse window will close, leaving the *Create Shortcut* window open.
3. Click *Next* and edit the name of the shortcut, if you want.
4. Click *Finish*.

If the target item is a program, rather than a folder or file, the method in option (4) is a bit tricky. That's because in order to open a program, you have to open the executable file. In most cases, the file that executes a program has an .exe file extension, and it can take a while to find among the many folders that a large program can have. And, if your preferences are set up to hide file extensions, forget it.

To make a shortcut to a program, try one of the options below.

(5) Via the Start menu, *Send to Desktop (create shortcut)*

1. Click on *Start* or *Start > All Programs* and find the program.
2. Find the icon/program name. If the program is listed as a folder, you'll have to drill down to the file that will open the program.

In Fig. 11-17, to make a shortcut to the program called Adobe Digital Editions, I clicked on *Start > All Programs > Adobe > Adobe Digital Editions 2.0* folder. Inside that folder were four programs. I right-clicked on the program called Adobe Digital Editions 2.0, and chose *Send to > Desktop (Create shortcut)*.

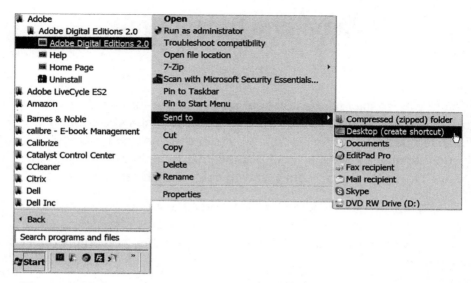

Fig. 11-17. Making a shortcut to a program that's inside a subfolder on the *Start > All Programs* menu in Windows 7.

Here are some other ways to make this shortcut to a program from the Start menu:

(6) **Right-click** on Adobe Digital Editions 2.0, **hold the button down, and drag the program to the desktop.** Let go of the button, choose *Create shortcut here,* OR

(7) **In Windows 7 (or Vista), right-click and choose *Pin to Start menu* or *Pin to Taskbar*** to put a shortcut in one of those locations, OR

(8) **In XP, right-click and choose *Create Shortcut.*** The program's shortcut would show up at the bottom of the All Programs menu with a (2) after it. Drag it out of *All Programs* and drop it on the Start menu, the taskbar, or the desktop. Rename the shortcut, OR

(9) **Right-click on the program and choose *Copy.*** Go to the new location, right-click, and choose *Paste Shortcut.*

If you're not sure you're making a shortcut to the correct file, just try it. Make the shortcut and then double-click on the shortcut to see what opens up. Delete the shortcut if it doesn't work.

Now, go to Chapter 13 and do Exercises 3, 4, and 5.

Mom and the Internet

Mom was so excited the first time we got on the Internet that she couldn't decide what to look up. Every few seconds she'd swing her excited gaze to meet mine, open her mouth to shout out her choice, and then just as abruptly shut it, shake her head in frustration, and say, "No, *wait* … I can come up with something better than *that*."

Sitting beside her, awaiting her decision as to what she wanted to see in this exciting new world, I felt a vainglorious sense of peace. *I* was providing my mother with the ability to do this, I thought smugly. It was all *me*.

Just then Mom practically leaped out of the chair, her decision made.

"Jared!" she shouted gleefully.

"What's Jared" I asked. I assumed it was a reference to the Biblical character, and I wasn't surprised. Mom had gone to church three times a week most of her life and it seemed fitting that the first thing she'd look up on the World Wide Web would have to do with God.

"What's Jared?" I gently prodded, knowing she wouldn't want to boast about her faith.

"Oh, for Heaven's sake," Mom said, rolling her eyes. "He's the young man I want to look *up*. You know … *Jared*. The boy who ate all those sandwiches and still lost weight!"

The world at her fingertips … (thanks to *me*!)

12 - The Internet

What is the Internet?

The Internet is a network of networks consisting of private, public, academic, business, and government computers linked by electronic, wireless, and optical technologies that use a standard set of protocols to relay and present data to users worldwide. Any computer can communicate with another computer if both are connected to the Internet.

Internet versus World Wide Web

The Internet is the linked network of computers. The World Wide Web is the information that can be accessed via the Internet.

Internet Service Provider (ISP)

An Internet Service Provider (often a telephone or cable company) provides fee-based access to the Internet through its servers. Connections to the Internet can be via telephone lines, cable modems, cellphones, and other mobile devices, according to the type of service you want and how much you're willing to pay.

TCP/IP and DNS

The Transmission Control Protocol and Internet Protocol (usually shown as TCP/IP) establish the rules for passing information through the Internet. Some of these rules include **IP addresses**—every device connected to the Internet has one—and a **Domain Name System (DNS)**. When you click on a website link, your ISP will route your request to a server further up the chain on the Internet; eventually the request will hit a DNS server. The DNS tries to resolve your website request to the correct IP address and if successful, sends your request directly there. If not, the request goes to another server further up the chain. Once the request reaches the correct server, packets of information are exchanged between that IP address and yours.

Uniform Resource Locator (URL)

A URL is a complete web address that takes the user to a page on the World Wide Web. It is usually made up of three parts:

1. Scheme
2. Host
3. Path

Scheme

The URL starts off with the scheme name, which signals that what follows can be interpreted with that protocol. The scheme in a URL is followed by a colon and two forward slashes. Two schemes are:

- **HTTP - HyperText Transfer Protocol** uses text connected by links to submit requests to a server and receive responses in return. This is the foundation of data communication for the World Wide Web. The URL would start with **http://** though you seldom have to actually type in the scheme these days.

- **FTP - File Transfer Protocol** allows users to transfer files to and from a server. FTP usually requires authentication (user and password). I use FTP to upload my website pages after I've edited them on my hard drive and to download copies from my website to my PC. The URL would start with **ftp://**

Host (AKA Domain Name)

The host, or domain name, is the second part of the URL. It's a string of characters separated by dots which resolves to an IP address. Domain names are generally easy to remember (google. com, microsoft.com, cbs.com), while IP addresses, which consist of numbers, are not. Domain names are not case sensitive. Typing in CNN.com will take you to the same place as cnn.com. (The same is true of email addresses.)

Historically, **www.** was required at the beginning of a domain name, but not anymore. Most sites are set up so that you will arrive at their domain name whether you type *www* in or not. There are still some websites that haven't done this mapping, though, so if you get a "Page Not Found" error for a website you're sure exists, try putting *www.* at the beginning of the domain name. Or try removing it.

The most important part of the domain name—to people who are searching for it, at least—is the name: **Amazon**.com, **CNN**.com, **BBC**.org, etc. The domain name can have several sections. The last section—called the top level domain—gives you information about the website. See some common top level domains below.

.com   commercial
.net   network
.org   non-profit organization
.edu   restricted to schools and educational organizations
.mil   restricted to U.S. military
.gov   restricted to U.S. government
.us   restricted to United States
.uk   restricted to the United Kingdom

Path

The third part of a URL, if a website has a third part, is the path. A URL's path follows a hierarchy and specifies a unique location, the same way a file path does in your PC. If you type *stephiesmith.com* into your browser Address bar, you'll go to the ***home*** page of my website. Anything added after the .com will take you to a specific location within that domain. *Stephiesmith.com/blog* will take you to my blog's main page. *Stephiesmith.com/2011/07/27/critters* will take you to a specific blog entry made on July 27, 2011, titled "I'll Take Florida, Critters and All."

Some website addresses end with the name of the item as does my *critters* page. Some end with .html, .htm, .php, .asp, etc. An image location may end with .jpg. A pdf document on the web will end with .pdf. And though the domain name is not case sensitive, the path may be, so if you are typing in a URL that someone wrote down for you, and it doesn't work, try changing the path letters to capital letters or vice versa.

Error 404 Page Not Found

The path of a URL is usually the culprit when you click to go to a website and get a 404 Error (page/file cannot be found). This is because people put pages in a particular location on their website and then they later change the storage location or the name of the page and forget to update all the links. If the path of the file stored on the website doesn't match the path of the code inserted into the link, the page can't be found.

Most website administrators set up a Redirect for these errors. The Redirect can take you to the new location of the page, back to the home page, or to a page with a message and/or a search box to search that website for the item you want.

When there is no redirect, and you're stuck on that Error 404 Page Not Found page, try these things:

(1) Check to make sure you have the entire URL pasted into the Address bar. Lots of people email a link and the link becomes broken during transmission. If the link is broken in an email, you'll see the link and then there will probably be a space or paragraph return, followed by nonsensical letters or numbers. Go back and get rid of the space or paragraph return and copy that link again (you may have to paste it into a Notepad document in order to delete the paragraph return and spaces), OR

(2) Start deleting sections of the file path starting from the right side. Delete the last section from the end to the first forward slash (/) you come to. Press enter and see what you get. Then delete the next section up to the next /. Press enter and see what you get. You may get a subsection of a website where you can figure out what to click on to get to where you want to go, or you may get an "access forbidden" warning. Eventually, you'll end up at the website's home page, OR

(3) Search for the page using a search engine such as Google.com.

Web Browsers

A web browser is a software program that translates and displays web pages. If you have an Internet connection and a web browser, you can access websites and interact with them.

A Windows PC comes with the Microsoft web browser—Internet Explorer (IE)—already installed. Other common web browsers are Google Chrome, Mozilla Firefox, and Apple Safari. You can install any or all of these browsers on your PC. I have IE, Chrome, and Firefox installed.

Why install more than one browser? Here are a few reasons:

- A particular browser might run slowly one day for whatever reason or have glitches from a software update.

- Websites can look different in different browsers, and a page may not load properly in one browser but will load fine in others.

- Most review sites say Google Chrome is the most secure browser. In general this is a good thing, but occasionally you may have trouble with a site that Chrome thinks you should stay away from.

Fig. 12-1. Google home page in the Google Chrome web browser. Some people love the minimalistic feel of Chrome (no menu bar); some hate it.

- Mozilla Firefox has a great ebook reader plug-in that will open an .epub format ebook if you click *File > Open File*. To install Mozilla Firefox and the epub plug-in, visit my website for detailed instructions at *http://stephiesmith.com/ereaders/firefox*

Fig. 12-2. Google home page in Mozilla Firefox web browser. According to my web user statistics, Firefox is used five to twenty times more than the other browsers visiting my website.

I suggest installing more than one browser. If you install Firefox, you can click on *Help > Firefox Help* and take their tutorial to learn the basics. In Google Chrome, click on the *Chrome Menu icon > Help* and start with "Take a tour of Chrome features." And if you do install other browsers, set up IE first so that you can import the IE settings into your other browsers to save time.

Internet Explorer (IE)

When you buy your PC or upgrade Windows, you'll get the latest version of IE available at that time. Then, unless you turn auto-updates off, IE will automatically update to the new version when it comes out. You can check your version by clicking *Help > About Internet Explorer,* and if there's a newer version available, you can click to install it.

Most of this information applies to IE version 10 (Fig. 12-3), because that's the current release at the time of writing this book.

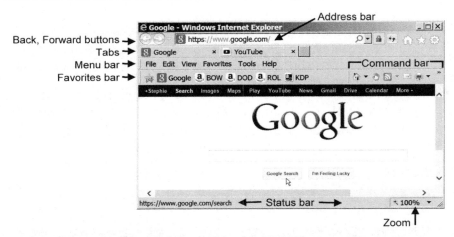

Fig. 12-3. The Google home page displayed in IE 10 in Windows 7.

Address bar give you the address (URL) of the website you're visiting or lets you type a website into it. If it's a website you've visited before, IE may assist you by completing the address, as well as give you a list of variations on the site in the drop-down menu. You can click on one of those or continue typing.

Back, Forward buttons take you back to the last page you visited and forward again.

Tabs represent the different pages you have open unless you've chosen to view every page in a window instead of a tab. You can click between tabs, reorder them, or drag one out and drop it onto the desktop.

Toolbars you can turn on or off

The IE toolbars are Menu bar, Favorites bar, Command bar, and Status bar. To turn these toolbars on or off (i.e., to make them show up or disappear), click on *View > Toolbars* and click to check or uncheck. Lock and unlock the toolbars from here too.

Menu bar is similar to any Windows menu bar and is comprised of File, Edit, View, Favorites, Tools, and Help. Click on each menu to see all the options. *File > Send > Link by email* will allow you to email someone (or yourself) the link to that page. Many items on these menus have a keyboard shortcut you can use.

For example, to open a new tab in IE, you can:

(1) Click *File > New tab,* OR

(2) Click on the empty square to the right of the open tab(s), OR

(3) Press Ctrl+T. See "IE Shortcuts" later in this chapter for a list.

Command bar gives you access to most of the same options and settings as the Menu bar. To customize the bar, right-click on it and choose *Customize > Add or Remove Commands.*

Status bar gives the status of the window you're in, i.e., what percent of the window has loaded, etc. If your windows load quickly and files download quickly, you may not see much in this bar in later versions of IE. In earlier versions, you may see a padlock, which signifies a secure site (this shows on the Address bar in later versions). You may also see the file path of links you mouse over on a website.

Favorites bar is where you place shortcuts (icons) to your favorite websites. If you have too many icons to fit on the bar, a chevron will appear. Click on the chevron to see the hidden icons, or to change the width of those showing. Drag the icons around to change their order, right-click to rename or delete, etc. To put a favorite on this bar, go to the website and drag the icon at the far left of the address bar down to the Favorites bar. When you see a vertical line, release the mouse. Then right-click on the icon to rename. See Fig. 12-4.

Fig. 12-4. Dragging a website icon down to the Favorites bar in IE 10.

Zoom and Text size

The **Zoom** feature enlarges or reduces *everything* on the page, whereas the **Text size** feature changes only the size of *text* (not images). Text that's been coded to a specific size cannot be changed via the Text size feature; in that case, *zoom* to enlarge. Once you change your zoom or text size on a page, all open pages switch to that too, as do any new pages or tabs you open thereafter.

There are a few ways to zoom:

(1) In the bottom right corner of the window (see Fig. 12-3), click *Zoom* and make your selection, OR

(2) On the Menu bar click *View > Zoom* and make your selection, OR

(3) With a keyboard, Ctrl+plus sign zooms in, Ctrl+minus sign zooms out, OR

(4) With a mouse, press Ctrl and move your thumbwheel up (zoom in) or down (zoom out), OR

(5) With a touchpad, start with two fingers together (like a pinch) and spread them apart to zoom in or move two fingers together (like a pinch) to zoom out.

Getting Around

There are many ways to get around in IE. Here are a few:

(1) **Click on a link.** The pointer/cursor turns into a hand when it encounters a clickable link, whether text or graphic. Some links will open in a new window or tab, some will open in the same window. It depends on how the website is coded, and how you have your browser set up (see *Tools > Internet Options > General tab > Tabs button*), OR

(2) **Use the Back and Forward arrows on the Address bar.** You have to visit some websites first before these arrows work, since the *Back* arrow takes you back to the last page you visited, and the *Forward* arrow brings you forward again, OR

(3) **Click on different windows or tabs.** Open a new tab by clicking on the little square to the right of the open tab(s) or press Ctrl+T. Click on a tab to switch to it or set your Internet Options up to always switch to a new tab. Open a new window with *File > New window* or press Ctrl+N. You can also drag a tab out of IE and drop it on the desktop to put it in its own window, OR

(4) **Click on a Favorite.** Microsoft sets up some favorites for you in the beginning; you set up the rest. Access them from the Favorites menu on the Menu bar or from the icons on the Favorites Bar, OR

(5) **From the drop-down menu to the right of the Address bar.** On the Address bar to the right of the magnifying glass is a triangle pointing down. Click on that to see URLs from recently visited places, OR

(6) **From the Explorer bar.** Under *View > Explorer bars*, you can choose *Favorites* or *History* or *Feeds* and a navigation pane will open on the left showing those items in three tabs. Click on a website from your history or favorites. In previous versions of IE, you can click on the Star icon showing at the top and the Favorites menu will open. It doesn't stay open, though, the way it does in IE 10's navigation pane, OR

(7) **From the IE jump list on the taskbar (Windows 7 only).** The Windows 7 jump list for a taskbar item is the list that pops

up when you right-click on the program icon. It may show you frequent or recent places, tasks you can do, etc.

Adding a Favorite

You can add a Favorite website to your *Favorites bar* as shown in Fig. 12-4, but you can also add it to your *list* of Favorites. See Fig. 12-5.

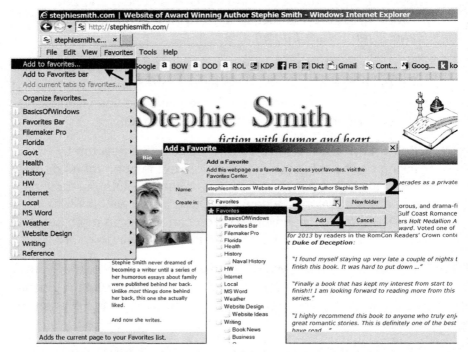

Fig. 12-5. Adding a favorite site to your Favorites list.

When you're on a web page you want to save to your Favorites:

[1]   Click on *Favorites > Add to favorites.*

[2]   A menu called "Add a Favorite" will open showing the name of the website. Click in that name to rename it as desired. It should be descriptive enough that you'll know what it is when you see it on your Favorites list.

[3]   If you have subject folders set up, click on the Favorites drop-down menu and click on the folder where you want the link to be saved. Otherwise skip to the next step.

[4]   Click *Add.*

To set up a folder in your Favorites, in step 3 above, click on the "New folder" button instead of the Favorites drop-down menu. A "Create a Folder" menu will open. Give the folder a name and click *Create*. (To put this folder inside another folder, click on the drop-down menu to the right of "Create in" and select the folder, then click *Create* and click *Add.)*

You can organize your Favorites at any time. Click *Favorites > Organize Favorites*. Drag the folders around or use the buttons to create a New Folder, or to Move, Rename, or Delete folders or websites.

Downloads

When you download a file, a window will pop up asking if you want to *download, download and install, download and open, save, save as,* etc.

If you're installing a program, it's easiest to select **Downstall and Install**. That way, the program will download and then automatically install for you.

If it's a document or file you want to open once, it's easiest to **Download and Open**. However, **if it's a document you want to save** it in a specific place so you can open it multiple times, choose **Download and Save As** and tell Windows where to save it. Either way, you can click on *Open* in the downloads notification box and Windows will open the file you just saved.

To see a list of downloads and where you've saved them, go to *Tools > View downloads* (or press Ctrl+J). You can change your default download location by clicking on *Options* in the lower left corner of this window and browsing to choose a different default location.

You can also save most files from the Internet by right-clicking on the file and choosing *Save Target as* or *Save picture as*, browsing to the location you want, and saving. These files will not be listed in the View Downloads folder though.

Never download a file or program from a website that you don't know to be safe!

Settings in Tools > Internet options

There are some settings you'll want to check and/or set up, especially if you plan to install another browser and transfer your settings.

Click on *Tools > Internet options.* There are several tabs on this menu. In IE 10 they are: General, Security, Privacy, Content, Connections, Programs, Advanced. See Fig. 12-6. I advise you to go through all tabs and options to see what's there.

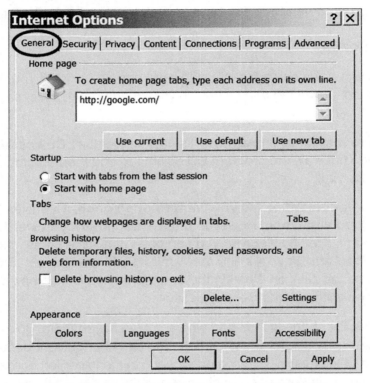

Fig. 12-6. The General tab of the Internet Options menu found under Tools on the Menu bar.

General tab

• **Set your home page.** This is the page you'll go to if you click the Home icon (looks like a house). It's also the page IE will open to if you so chose. The easiest way to set your home page is to close out the menu and go to the website page you want to set as your home page. Then open *Tools > Internet options > General tab* and under the *Home page* options, click on the *Use current* button.

The next option is *Startup* where you choose to start with this home page or to reopen the tabs from your last browsing session.

- **Tabs > Tab button.** If you click on the Tabs button on the General tab, the Tabbed Browsing Settings menu opens. Fig. 12-7 shows my settings.

Fig. 12-7. Menu at *Tools > Internet Options > General tab > Tabs > Tabbed Browsing Settings.*

- **Browsing History.** Here's where you decide how often you want IE to check for a new version of a page, how many days of history you want saved, etc.

- **Appearance.** You can decide how to view pages that haven't specified particular fonts, colors, etc.

Security Tab

In the box at the top, click on each icon (Internet, Local Intranet, Trusted Sites, Restricted Sites) to select settings for that zone (see Fig. 12-8).

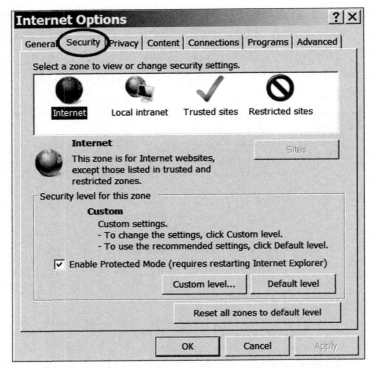

Fig. 12-8. *Tools > Internet Options > Security tab.* The *Internet zone* is selected at the top in the rectangular box, so the other settings showing on this tab will apply to that zone while it is selected.

Internet zone. Generally you'll want to go with a Medium-high default setting and then see what happens. Click the box to *Enable Protected Mode* if it's available; it's an extra layer of protection against sites that try to invade your computer with malicious code. I use a custom level that's close to the medium-high default with a few exceptions. You can click on *Custom level* to see the different options. If you make changes to your Internet settings, click *Apply* before continuing to another zone.

You can view a chart comparing IE security levels at this link (hopefully this link will remain on this website):

http://blogs.technet.com/b/steriley/archive/2008/09/16/internet-explorer-security-levels-compared.aspx

Local Intranet zone is your corporate or business network (note this is IntRAnet, not IntERnet). Click the Sites button and select the option "Automatically detect Intranet network" so your business network, if you have one set up, will be detected. The default for the local **intranet** settings is usually Medium.

Trusted sites zone. These are sites you specifically put here because you are sure they can be trusted. At work we have a Windows SharePoint Services (WSS) site that we use to exchange information, so I have this site in my Trusted sites zone.

Restricted sites are sites you specifically tell Windows not to trust.

Privacy tab lets you choose your Cookie settings and whether or not to allow pop-up windows.

• Cookies are small text files that a website downloads to your computer. In the Privacy tab you can choose a level for cookies, then click on *Advanced* where you'll see more settings. First party cookies are cookies from the website you're visiting and you usually want to allow those (otherwise you can't bank or shop online or have your user names and passwords saved). Third-party cookies are from other websites, many of which are tracking information for marketing purposes. You can turn those off and see how much trouble you have navigating sites.

• Pop-ups are windows that pop up while you're on a website (these are not windows that open when you click on a link). Block pop-ups because most are not needed and some are downright unsafe. If you're on a site that can't perform a task because you've blocked pop-ups, the site should put a message on the screen that you need to enable your pop-ups. Click on *Tools > Pop-up blocker* and turn it off temporarily or change the settings for that site.

Content tab lets you choose settings for Auto Complete and RSS Feeds. ***Auto Complete* stores entries you've made and suggests matches for you.** It includes websites, searches, favorites, feeds, etc. Choose whether or not to have IE automatically save your user names and passwords and complete Forms for you. If your computer is shared with someone else, you might not want your passwords saved automatically or to have forms filled in automatically with your information. If you don't usually share your computer but may have a guest staying for a while, you can go into this tab and delete all your auto complete information and tell IE to ask you before storing user names and passwords. For RSS feeds, see next section.

Connections tab lets you set up internet and network connections.

Programs tab lets you choose IE as your default web browser, manage your add-on programs, and set programs for opening various types of files on the Internet. You can probably skip this. If you aren't able to open a file on the Internet, you should be asked to assign a program to it then.

Advanced tab has additional settings. Some of these further define other selections you've made. Go through them. There are only a couple of these that I changed. I told IE to always underline links, to notify me when downloads are complete, and to automatically recover from page layout errors with Compatibility View (Compatibility View may not be available in earlier versions of IE).

What is an RSS feed?

Really Simple Syndication (RSS) feeds provide blog or news feed updates. If a feed is available on a site, the feed button in the Command bar is orange. Click on the feed button to see what info is offered in the feed and click to *Subscribe to this feed* (near the top left of the web page).

IE shortcuts

Look through these shortcuts for actions you perform often where using a keyboard shortcut might save you time.

Tab shortcuts

Ctrl+Tab - switch between tabs
Ctrl+T - open a new tab
Ctrl+Shift+T - reopen the last tab you closed
Ctrl+W - close tabs
Ctrl+Shift+P - open a new InPrivate Browsing tab

Address bar shortcuts

Ctrl+Enter - add *www.* to the beginning and *.com* to the end of text typed in the Address bar

Alt+D - select the text in the Address bar
F4 - display a list of addresses you've typed

Browsing shortcuts

Alt+Home - go to your home page
Page up - move up a page
Page down - move down a page
Esc - stop downloading a page
F1 - get help & support
F5 - refresh page
F11 - toggle between full-screen and regular views
Ctrl+F - find something on this page
Ctrl+H - open browsing history
Ctrl+J - view downloads
Ctrl+Shift+Delete - delete browsing history

Favorites, history, and feeds shortcuts

Alt+Up arrow - move selected item up in the Favorites list (in the Organize Favorites dialog box)
Alt+Down arrow - move selected item down in the Favorites list (ditto)
Alt+A - open the Favorites menu from the menu bar
Alt+Z - open the Add to favorites menu
Ctrl+B - open the Organize Favorites dialog box
Crtl+D - add current site to favorites
Ctrl+G - view feeds
Ctrl+H - view history

Add-ons

Add-ons are programs that you can add to your browser. To see them or search for them, click on the drop-down menu on the right side of the Address bar and click on *Add* at the bottom. Be aware that add-ons will slow down your browser and most of the add-ons available through IE won't be worth that. Most of them simply allow you to add their button to your browser so you can click to go to their website. Since you have the ability to add buttons to your Favorites bar or list, that isn't needed.

13 - Exercises

Try the exercises without looking at the solutions. (Note: To partici-
pate in the exercises, your mouse must open items with a double
click.)

Close any open windows.

Exercise 1 - Moving your taskbar around

1. Move your taskbar to the left side of your desktop.
2. Move it to the top of your desktop.
3. Move it to the right side.
4. Move it back to the bottom of your screen.

Exercise 2 - Manipulating open windows

1. Open the Recycle Bin using any method; open My Computer/
    Computer using a different method; and open a third window
    (e.g., Control Panel, Documents, Internet Explorer) using yet
    another method.
2. You should have 3 windows open on your desktop. Auto-arrange
    them in a Cascade style. Activate each window in turn so that it
    moves to the front.
3. Manually resize and move the three open windows so they are
    different sizes and fill the screen as much as possible. Make one
    stretch across the screen horizontally or vertically. Fit the other
    two in the remaining area.
4. Make the three windows disappear from the desktop without
    closing them, then make them all reappear.
5. Resize one of the windows until a scroll bar appears. Use the
    scroll bar or mouse to view the contents of that window. Try
    moving the spacer as well as clicking on different empty parts of
    the scroll bar.
6. Maximize the window you resized, then restore it.
7. Have Windows auto arrange all windows horizontally, then put
    them back as they were.
8. Close the windows using three different methods.

Exercise 3 - Opening and using a Windows program

1. Open the Paint program.
2. Take a screen shot of your desktop and paste it into Paint.
3. Maximize the Paint window and draw a circle around the My Computer/Computer icon on the picture of your desktop. (If you can't see Computer in the screen shot, circle something else.)
4. Type "This is a screen shot of my desktop" anywhere on the picture. (Hint: The text tool is usually represented by a large "A.")
5. Save the picture as a jpg file and call it *MyDesktop* and close Paint.

Exercise 4 - Searching for a file and changing its location

1. Search for the jpg file *MyDesktop*. If you already know where it is, search anyway.
2. Open the file in Paint and save it to your desktop. (If it's already saved to the desktop, save it somewhere else.)
3. Search for the file again, find the one that is NOT stored on the desktop, and delete it.

Exercise 5 - Creating, moving, renaming, and deleting files/folders and making shortcuts

1. Create a new folder inside the My Documents folder. Name it "Exercise 5."
2. Move the *MyDesktop* file from your desktop to the Exercise 5 folder.
3. Drag the Exercise 5 folder from your My Documents folder and drop it into your My Pictures folder.
4. Make a shortcut to the *MyDesktop* picture and put the shortcut on your desktop.
5. Delete the shortcut.
6. Delete the Exercise 5 folder using a different method than used in Step 5 above.

Exercise 6 - Navigating the Internet

1. Open IE and open a new tab.
2. Type "google.com" into the Address bar (if google.com is your

home page, type msn.com) and press Enter.

3.   Change the zoom level to 150%.

4.   Pin this site to your Favorites bar, open a new tab and click on the Google (or MSN) icon that you just pinned to your Favorites bar to go there again.

5.   Type "youtube" into the Google search box and click on a link to go to _YouTube.com_. Search for something fun, and chances are you'll find YouTube videos of that item. I just now searched for "singing donkey," and yes, I found videos of singing donkeys.

6.   Drag the YouTube tab out of IE and drop it on the desktop.

7.   Open each of these in a new tab: Yahoo.com, MSN.com, Amazon.com.

8.   Open your history window and see what shows there. Use the drop-down menu to display/sort in different ways.

9.   Close each tab/window separately and close IE.

Exercise 7 - Download a web file from a site, revisit a site

1.   Go to the U.S. Internal Revenue Service website.

2.   Find their downloadable pdf file called "Farmer's Tax Guide" (Publication 225).

3.   Save a copy to your computer, open it, and close it.

4.   Close out IE completely, then reopen IE.

5.   Revisit the IRS website without either typing in the URL or using a search engine.

14 - Exercise Solutions

SOLUTION 1

1. *Move your taskbar to the left side of your desktop.*
2. *Move it to the top of your desktop.*
3. *Move it to the right side.*
4. *Move it back to the bottom of your screen.*

This involves *Drag and Drop* (Chapter 3). Click on an empty area of the taskbar and, while keeping your mouse button pressed down, drag the bar to the new location and then release the mouse button. Do that for each position.

SOLUTION 2

1. *Open the Recycle Bin using any method; open My Computer/ Computer using a different method; and open a third window (e.g., Control Panel, Documents, Internet Explorer) using yet another method.*

- Double-click, OR
- Single-click and press *Enter*, OR
- Right-click, then click *Open*, OR
- Click on the Start button and select the item to open, or click on the Start button, right-click on the item and click *Open*.

2. *You should have 3 windows open on your desktop. Auto- arrange them in a Cascade style. Activate each window in turn so that it moves to the front.*

- Right-click on an empty area of your taskbar, then click on *Cascade Windows*.
- To activate each window, just click somewhere on the window or click on the Window name on the taskbar. The window will move to the front.

3. *Manually resize and move the three open windows so they are different sizes and fill the screen as much as possible. Make one stretch across the screen horizontally or vertically. Fit the*

other two in the remaining area.

Move each window to a corner of your screen by clicking on an empty area of the title bar and dragging (Chapter 3). Resize the windows one at a time (Chapter 7). Since you want to fill the screen, you might do something similar to Fig. 14-1.

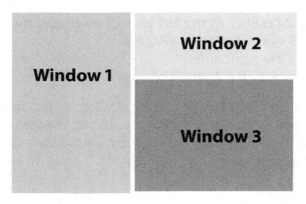

Fig. 14-1. Three Windows resized to fill the screen.

4. Make the three windows disappear from the desktop without closing them, then make them all reappear.

- Click on *Show Desktop* to make windows disappear and then click on it again to make them reappear, OR
- Right-click on taskbar and choose *Show Desktop*, and then right-click on taskbar and choose *Show Open Windows* or *Undo* (whatever is available), OR
- Click on the Minimize button on each window, then click on each window to restore (Chapter 7).

5. Resize one of the windows until a scroll bar appears. Use the scroll bar or mouse to view the contents of that window. Try moving the spacer as well as clicking on different empty parts of the scroll bar.

Resize the window smaller until scroll bars show up. Then practice scrolling by clicking on the up arrow, down arrow, and the depressed areas (Chapter 7).

6. Maximize the window you resized, then restore it.

- To maximize, click on the Maximize button, OR double-click on the title bar. In Windows 7 you can also drag the window to the top of the screen.

- To restore the window back to its original location, click on the Restore button, OR double-click on the title bar again, OR (in Windows 7) drag the window downward.

7. Have Windows auto arrange all windows horizontally, then put them back as they were.

To auto arrange horizontally, right-click on the taskbar and choose *Show Windows Stacked* or *Tile Windows Horizontally.* Right-click on the taskbar and choose *Undo.*

8. Close the windows using three different methods.

- Click on the X in upper right corner of the folder, OR
- Right-click on the title bar and click *Close,* OR
- Click on File menu (if one is showing) and click *Close,* OR
- Right-click on the item on the taskbar and either click *Close* or click on the X.

SOLUTION 3

OK, so I threw in some things we didn't exactly go over, but my goal is to help you learn to figure things out, so I hope you tried.

1. Open the Paint program.

You may have found Paint on your Start menu, or in *Start > All Programs,* or pinned to your taskbar (Chapter 9). I couldn't find the Paint program in any of those places, so I had to search for it (Chapter 11).

2. Take a screen shot of your desktop and paste it into Paint.

Press the Print Sceen button to take a picture of your desktop, then click inside the Paint window and either type Ctrl+V or right-click and choose Paste (Chapter 9). Whatever was on your desktop at the time you took the screen shot will be in the picture, so if the Paint program was open, it will be in there. (Note: devices without a Print Screen, PRTSC, or PRTSCN button usually have a different key combination to accomplish this, such as FN+Insert key. Check your manual.)

3. Maximize the Paint window and draw a circle around the My

Computer/Computer icon on the picture of your desktop. (If you can't see Computer in the screen shot, circle something else.)

Click on the maximize icon (Chapter 7) of the Paint window so that you can see all the paint tools. Click on the Home tab if you're not on that tab already, and click on the Circle in the Shapes box. Draw a circle around Computer (or something else).

4. Type "This is a screen shot of my desktop" anywhere on the picture. (Hint: The text tool is usually represented by a large "A.")

Click on the text tool and click anywhere on the picture of the desktop and type the words, "This is a screen shot of my desktop."

5. Save the picture as a jpg file and call it MyDesktop and close Paint.

Click on the icon to the left of the Home tab or click on the icon that looks like a square disk (represents a floppy disk) above that. Either of those will open a menu that will let you save the file as a jpg/jpeg file (you may have to click on the drop-down menu to choose jpg as the file type) (Chapter 11). Name the file *MyDesktop*. Click Save and close Paint.

OK, in this step you had to take a leap of faith because you might not have recognized the icon to the left of the Home tab. But if you thought about it, the File menu that allows you to save files is usually in this location, so it makes sense to click on that icon to see what it does. Even if you didn't think of that, you had to look for a menu that would allow you to save the file, OR maybe you remembered that the keyboard shortcut for Save is Ctrl+S. Don't be afraid to try things.

SOLUTION 4

1. Search for the jpg file MyDesktop. If you know where it is, search anyway.

Search for the file (Chapter 11 for all steps).

2. Open the file in Paint and save it to your desktop.

Right-click on the file name and choose *Open with* and select *Paint*. Click on *Save as* and browse to the desktop to save it. (If you double-clicked to open the file and Windows opened it in Windows Picture Viewer or some other program, I hope you closed the program and then thought to right-click and choose *Open with* Paint as mentioned above. Whenever something doesn't happen the way you expect it to, always recall your basic Windows skills to figure out what to do.)

3. Search for the file again, find the one that is NOT stored on the desktop, and delete it.

Same search but this time, in XP, look under the Folder column that shows the locations of the search results to find the original file NOT stored on the desktop. In Windows 7, search and click *See more results* to open the Search Results folder.

In both versions, click on the original file and press the Delete key (or right-click on it, and select *Delete*).

SOLUTION 5

1. Create a new folder inside the My Documents folder. Name it "Exercise 5."

There are many ways to do this.

- You can create the folder on your desktop (right-click, choose *New folder*, name it *Exercise 5*), then copy/paste or drag and drop it in the My Documents folder, OR
- go to the My Documents folder and create the new folder there.

You can also get to your My Documents folder in several different ways:

- from the Start menu, OR
- from Start > Search, OR
- from your desktop if you have a shortcut, OR
- from your Computer icon *(Computer > Local disk (C:) > Users > Your username > My Documents)*, OR
- from any folder using the Folders Pane in XP or the Navigation Pane in Windows 7; you may have to expand the folders in the Folders/Navigation pane (Chapter 11 for all steps).

2. Move the MyDesktop file from your Desktop to the Exercise 5 folder.

You can use Windows Explorer to navigate to the Exercise 5 folder or use one of the methods described in step 1. If using Windows Explorer:

1. Open any folder and click on *Desktop* in the Navigation Pane.
2. In the folder contents area, right-click on the *MyDesktop* picture and choose *Cut* (Ctrl+X).
3. Then either click on your My Documents folder in the Folders/ Navigation Pane (in Windows 7 you may need to click on *Libraries > Documents > My Documents*) and then double click on the Exercise 5 folder, OR expand the My Documents folder in the Folders view/Navigation Pane, and then click on the Exercise 5 subfolder.
4. The Exercise 5 folder should be open. In the folder contents area, right-click and choose Paste (Ctrl+V).

3. Drag the Exercise 5 folder from your My Documents folder and drop it into your My Pictures folder.

You need to be able to see both the Exercise 5 folder and the My Pictures folder, either using the Folders view/Navigation Pane (you may need to expand the folders) or by opening each folder in its own window. Then drag the Exercise 5 folder into the My Pictures folder.

4. Make a shortcut to the MyDesktop picture and put the shortcut on your desktop.

The easiest way is to navigate to the Exercise 5 folder contents or open the folder, then right-click on the *MyDesktop* picture and choose *Send to > Desktop (create shortcut).* OR you can make the shortcut and drag it to the desktop.

5. Delete the shortcut.

- Click on the shortcut and press the Delete key, OR
- Right-click on the shortcut and choose Delete, OR
- Drag it to the Recycle Bin.

6. Delete the Exercise 5 folder using a different method than used in Step 5 above.

SOLUTION 6

1. Open IE and open a new tab.

Click on the New Tab square to the right of the tab that's open OR press Ctrl+T.

2. Type "google.com" into the Address bar (if google.com is your home page, type msn.com) and press Enter.

Click in the Address bar. The URL that's in there should be high-lighted so that you can type google.com, replacing the current URL. Press Enter.

3. Change the zoom level to 150%.

- Click *View > Zoom > 150%*, OR
- Click Zoom in the bottom right-hand side of the page and choose 150%, OR
- Hold down the Ctrl key and (1) press the + sign, OR (2) move the thumbwheel upward on your mouse, OR (3) with your touchpad, do whatever constitutes scrolling up.

4. Pin this site to your Favorites bar, open a new tab and click on the Google (or MSN) icon that you just pinned to your Favorites bar to go there again.

Drag the URL icon at the left of the Address bar down to your Favorites bar and drop it. Right-click on it to rename it. Click on the New Tab square to the right of the current tab (or press Ctrl+T). Click on the Google favorite icon on your Favorites bar to open another Google page.

5. Type "youtube" into the Google search box and click on a link to go to YouTube.com. Search for something that seems ridiculous.

Type youtube in the search box and press enter. Choose a link that looks like it will go to the YouTube website and click on it. Search for something.

6. Drag the YouTube tab out of IE and drop it on the desktop.

Click on the YouTube tab and drag it away from IE and drop it on the desktop. Now you'll have two separate windows open in IE, and one will probably have multiple tabs.

7. Open each of these in a new tab: Yahoo.com, MSN.com, Amazon.com.

Choose either of the open IE windows, open a new tab, and type yahoo.com in the Address bar. Do the same for msn.com and amazon.com.

8. Open your history window and see what is there. Use the drop-down menu to display/sort in different ways.

- Click *View > Explorer bars > History*, OR
- Click on the *Star icon > History tab*

Once you have the History tab open, click on the drop-down menu at the top and change the view. Options will include *View by most visited*, View by date, *View by site*, etc. Scroll to see everything in there.

9. Close each tab/window separately and close IE.

- Click on the X in each tab window, OR
- Click *File > Close tab*, OR
- Click on the taskbar and click in the X, or right-click and choose *Close.*

SOLUTION 7

1. Go to the U.S. Internal Revenue Service website.

Search for IRS in Google.com OR type irs.gov into your address bar and hit enter. (Chapter 12 for all steps.)

2. Find the downloadable pdf file called "Farmer's Tax Guide" (Publication 225).

On the irs.gov website, search for *225* or *farmers tax guide*.

3. Save a copy to your computer, open it, and close it.

Sometimes when you click to save a file from the browser's *File > Save as* menu or when you right-click on the file and choose *Save Target as,* you may notice that Windows is saving the file as an html file. This isn't convenient for saving pdf files. So:

- Click on the link instead. You'll go to another web page where you will see "Publication 225 (HTML)," shown as two links. Mouse over each of those links and you'll see in the Status bar (bottom of window) that the *Publication 225* link ends with pdf. If you right-click and *Save Target as*, you'll be able to save a PDF file, OR

- Click on Publication 225 to open the file. On the far left you'll see the "Save" icon (rectangular floppy disk). Click on that to save the PDF file. When you save a file from the Internet this way, always pay attention to the location where Windows saves it.
- Open the file on your hard drive and then close it.

4. Close out IE completely, then reopen IE.

Close all IE windows and tabs so that none show on the taskbar.

5. Revisit the IRS website without typing in the URL or using a search engine.

- Right-click on the IE icon on the taskbar to see if the IRS site shows up in the jump list that pops up, OR click on *Reopen Last Session*, OR
- Open IE and click on the Address bar drop-down triangle and look for irs.gov and click, OR
- Open IE and open the History window. Look at history for *Today*, click on irs.gov, and choose one of the pages to click on.

15 - Questions & Answers

Mouse and Touchpad

QUESTION: My mouse doesn't act right. Icons appear to be selected when I move the mouse cursor over them, but nothing happens to my open windows when I do the same thing.

ANSWER: Your mouse is set up to open items with a single click, so the act of moving your cursor over the item causes the item to be selected so that a single click will open it. If you don't like this, follow instructions in Chapter 3 to change back to opening items with a double click.

QUESTION: My mouse is set for double-clicking, but sometimes things open when I haven't even clicked once.

ANSWER: First, check your Start menu properties for a choice that says "Open submenus when I pause on them with the mouse pointer." This setting is under the *Customize* button on the Start menu tab (and then you may have to also click on "Advanced"). Make sure that option is not checked. But I have this problem in Vista some-times, and that option is not checked. The last time it happened I switched to single-clicking to open items and then changed back to double-clicking and it stopped. But I might have been lucky.

QUESTION: If I start to drag the wrong folder, is there a way to cancel in the middle of dragging?

ANSWER: If you're dragging with the left mouse button, press your Esc (Escape) key, located in the upper left corner of your keyboard, and then let go of the mouse button. If you're dragging with your right mouse button, let go, and when the right-click menu opens, click *Cancel*. You can also right-click and choose *Undo* after the action is completed.

QUESTION: When I click on a folder selection that has a cascading menu, I have trouble selecting the correct item because other menus open. I keep having to start over, even when I'm trying to select something from the Start menu.

ANSWER: I think the problem you're having has to do with the way you move your mouse over to the cascading menu. People have a tendency to move their mouse down or diagonally instead of straight across and then down. When you click on the arrow pointing right (beside the first item) and the next tier appears, move your mouse directly to the right until it's in the middle of the top row of the cascading menu, and then move down the list until you get to the arrow for the next tier. Repeat those actions for each tier until you get to the item you want to open.

As far as the Start menu goes, if you find this to be a problem, you can customize your Start menu properties so that items such as your Control Panel, Documents, etc., open as a link, which means a new window, rather than a cascading menu, will open.

QUESTION: When I click on an icon to drag it, the name of the icon gets highlighted and I can't move it anywhere.

ANSWER: You have accidentally clicked on the name, not the icon. If you click on the name, Windows thinks you want to rename the item, and your mouse cursor turns into a text cursor. Press the Esc key, then try again.

QUESTION: I prefer double-clicking to open items, but half the time when I double-click, nothing happens.

ANSWER: Change the amount of time between the two clicks. If there's too much time between them, Windows interprets them as two single clicks. The double-click speed can be changed on the Buttons tab of the Mouse Properties menu.

QUESTION: Sometimes Windows *copies* an item when I drag with the left button, even though I don't hold down the Ctrl key. How can I force it to *move* the item, rather than move a copy of it?

ANSWER: This usually happens when you're moving an item to another disk. You can force Windows to move the item without copying it by pressing the Shift key before dragging.

QUESTION: I wanted to change my XP mouse pointer to a bigger one, but I don't get the choices you show in your example. In fact, I don't get any choices.

ANSWER: Go to your Control Panel, then to *Add or Remove Programs*, and click on *Add/Remove Windows Components*. If there's a component called *Accessories and Utilities*, click on the *Details* button. Then click on *Accessories* and click on *Details* again. Several items should be listed, one of them *Mouse Pointers*. You can add pointers from there.

QUESTION: Sometimes I have to pick up my mouse or move it around a lot to get it to work.

ANSWER: First, check a couple of settings in the Mouse Properties menu. Make sure the *Enhance Pointer Precision* option (under the Pointer Options tab) is not turned on. It's supposed to make your mouse more precise, but it can make your mouse slow. While you're there make sure your pointer speed isn't too slow.

If a light is shining out of your mouse, you have an optical mice. These use light sensors, so if yours is giving you trouble, make sure there's no extraneous light shining on or around it.

If it's not an optical mouse, turn the mouse over to see if there's a round hole with a rubber ball inside. If so, the mouse may need cleaning. Unplug the mouse, turn the ring counter-clockwise to open it and take out the ball. Wipe it off. Now look inside the mouse at the three rollers. Dirt usually collects in a line around the middle of each roller. Dislodge the dirt using a letter opener, your fingernail, a tooth-pick, etc. Then use a Q-tip with a little rubbing alcohol to remove the rest of the dirt. Turn the mouse over again and shake it gently in case any dirt fell back in. When everything is clean and dry, replace the ball, screw the ring back on and plug in the mouse. You may have to restart your PC for it to recognize the mouse.

If all else fails, try a different mouse, even if you have to borrow one temporarily. If the borrowed mouse works, buy another mouse. They don't last forever.

QUESTION: I like using the thumbwheel to scroll, but it goes too fast.

ANSWER: Go to the Control Panel and open the Mouse Properties folder. Click on Wheel and type in a lesser number of lines for the mouse to scroll at a time, or move the slider closer to *Slow* if that's the kind of adjustment you have.

QUESTION: When I use my thumbwheel on the Internet, the pointer changes to a two-headed symbol and the page moves up and down by itself.

ANSWER: You pushed down on the thumbwheel before you started scrolling. That activates a special feature called *auto scroll* that some mice with thumbwheels have. Push on the thumbwheel again or click with your left button to de-activate auto scroll. To use the auto scroll, move your mouse up or down without touching the thumbwheel. To control how fast the auto scroll goes, adjust your mouse settings.

QUESTION: Just moving my hands near the touchpad makes the cursor move around in my documents and sometimes closes what I'm working on. Is there a setting I can change, or a way I can turn the touchpad off and just use the mouse?

ANSWER: The solution may lie in either the hardware or software, and there may be options for disabling and/or adjusting settings.

Hardware: (1) Some laptops and notebooks (newer ones, particularly) have a physical switch located on the laptop's edge, so first look for that. Make sure you're not turning off your wireless capability, though, because that switch can be on the edge of your laptop too, OR (2) Alternatively, your brand of laptop may offer a keyboard shortcut to disable the touchpad, or may allow you to tap a certain area of the touchpad to turn it off. Check your laptop's documentation or go to the manufacturer's website and search for the information.

Software: (1) Check your Notification area, including the hidden icons, for a touchpad icon. If you have one, open it and adjust the settings or look for the option to disable it. (2) If you don't have that icon, go to *Control Panel > Mouse Properties > Touchpad* (or *Control Panel > Hardware and Sound > Mouse > Touchpad*) and adjust those settings. (3) If there are no options for a touchpad in your Mouse properties, it may be a separate software. Search for it (see Chapter 11). (4) If you don't find anything, search for "device manager" and expand *Mice and other pointing devices*. Right-click the touchpad option and click *Disable*. (5) Finally, you can download a third party software such as Touchpad Pal, which will disable the touchpad whenever it detects that you are typing and reenable the touchpad when you're done.

Recycle Bin

QUESTION: I tried to open something in the Recycle Bin and nothing happened.

ANSWER: You can't open an item while it's in the Recycle Bin. You have to get it out of the Recycle Bin first. If you want to file the item back where it was, right-click on the item in the Recycle Bin and select Restore. If you just want to take a look at it, drag it out onto your desktop and open it. Then you can drag it back to the Bin. Note: If you Restore something after you've dragged it out to the Desktop and then back to the bin, the item will be restored to the Desktop because that's the last place it was.

QUESTION: When I open my Recycle Bin, I don't see any of the information like in your screen shot where it shows the Date Deleted. I'd like to see that plus the Creation Date of the file I deleted.

ANSWER: You need to be in *Details View* of the folder to see the details of the items in the Recycle Bin. After you're in the Details View, you may have to change the columns that are showing, as well as the order they are in, to see the details you want. See Chapter 10.

QUESTION: When I drag something to the Recycle Bin, the item just sits on top of the bin and doesn't go in.

ANSWER: When you drag something to the Recycle Bin, make sure that the Recycle Bin becomes highlighted (selected) as you move the item over it—before you let go of the mouse button. Otherwise, the item won't go in. Remember you can also select the item you're trying to delete and just press the Delete key to send it to the Recycle Bin.

QUESTION: I know I deleted a folder some time ago and I have never emptied my Recycle Bin (ever!) but it's not in there. What happened to it and how can I get it back?

ANSWER: You can't get back the things Windows already deleted from the Recycle Bin. As for what happened, if the items in your Recycle Bin take up more than ten percent of your hard disk space, Windows starts deleting the oldest items. You can change this for the future by right-clicking on the Recycle Bin, clicking on Properties on the menu that appears, and changing the percentage to more than ten percent. Or, periodically delete items you're sure you won't want again from your Recycle Bin so that the items don't take up ten percent of your hard disk space.

Start/Logon/Shutdown

QUESTION: When I click on the Start button, all the programs pop up and I can't get to, or even see, the other things on the menu.

ANSWER: The program menu will appear if you move your mouse too slowly over the words *All Programs* on the Start menu. Press your Esc key to close that menu and move your mouse pointer down below the All Programs link until you know what you want to click on.

QUESTION: Every time I click on my Start menu I get a large message that says there are too many items to show them all. How can I make that message quit showing up?

ANSWER: Follow the instructions that show up under that message. You can customize your Start menu to show smaller icons or to display fewer of your most often-used programs, or you can unpin/remove some of the items you don't want there by right-clicking on those items and selecting "Remove from this list."

QUESTION: Is there a way I can close my laptop lid without Windows shutting down?

ANSWER: Yes. That option is located in *Control Panel > Power Options* in both XP and Windows 7. Click on the Advanced tab of the Power Options menu, look for "When I close the lid of my portable computer," and choose the option "Do nothing," click *Apply* and *OK*. In Windows 7 you may also be able to get to this setting from *Personalize > Screen Saver > Change Power Settings*.

Taskbar

QUESTION: I can't get the taskbar to move. I can't even get a two-headed arrow so that I can try to resize the taskbar.

ANSWER: Your taskbar is locked. Right-click on the taskbar and click on *Lock the Taskbar* to remove the checkmark and unlock it.

QUESTION: My taskbar has disappeared.

ANSWER: Try these things. First minimize all your open windows.

(1) Look carefully at the perimeter of your screen for a thin line the color of your taskbar. If you see the thin line, move your mouse over it until you get the 2-headed arrow and drag toward the center of your screen. If that works, then your taskbar was dragged off the screen. (2) If you don't see the edge of the taskbar, move your mouse pointer around the perimeter of your screen to see if the taskbar suddenly appears. If it does, then it's set to "Auto Hide" which means that it disappears unless you point to it. Point to it to make it appear, right-click on an empty area and uncheck *Auto Hide*. While you're in the taskbar menu, make sure the option for keeping the taskbar on top of other windows is checked. Even if you decide you like the auto hide feature, you will still want the taskbar to stay on top. Otherwise, if you have a window filling the screen, your taskbar will be hidden.

If your taskbar disappears more often than you'd like, lock it in place by right-clicking on it and choosing *Lock the Taskbar*. You will have to unlock it, though, to make any changes to it.

QUESTION: When I try to move my taskbar, it just gets taller.

ANSWER: You are resizing it rather than moving it. This can happen if your mouse pointer is too close to the edge of the taskbar when you click to drag and drop. Being close to the edge can cause the pointer to turn into a two-headed resizing arrow, which you might not have noticed. Make sure your mouse pointer is smack in the middle of an empty area on the taskbar before you click to drag the taskbar to another location.

QUESTION: I want to cascade all my open windows but I can't find an empty place on the taskbar to click on unless I close windows first, and I don't want to do that.

ANSWER: You can either drag the taskbar upwards to make it taller until an empty area shows up, or you can right-click on the Clock, if it's showing on your Notification Area. The clock is the only taskbar item you can right-click on that will give you the same menu as clicking on an empty area of the taskbar.

QUESTION: Sometimes I right-click on an item on the taskbar, like the Volume control, and a menu for something else pops up.

ANSWER: Possibly you weren't exactly on top of the Volume control when you right-clicked, but sometimes this just happens. The easiest way out is to press your Esc key and the menu will disappear. Then try again.

QUESTION: I want to make a window active but I can't see it at all.

ANSWER: Look for the window on your taskbar and click on it to bring it to the front of your desktop. OR right-click on the taskbar and click on *Cascade Windows*. If the window is open on your desktop, it will show up. OR hold down the Alt key and keep pressing the Tab key until the window shows up. If none of these tricks work, the window isn't open anymore.

QUESTION: I want to resize my taskbar to make it double in height, but even though I get the two-headed arrow, I can't resize it upward. And the taskbar isn't locked.

ANSWER: You have a window maximized on your screen or you have all your windows stacked, which fills up the screen. The taskbar can only expand if there's room on the desktop, so minimize or restore any full screen windows before you try to resize the taskbar.

QUESTION: I closed all windows by clicking on the X's, but one of them still shows on the taskbar even though it's not on my desktop.

ANSWER: Sometimes this happens, especially with pop-up ads from the Internet. Right-click on the item on the taskbar and select Close. You may want to check and make sure you're using the Pop-up Blocker on the Internet.

QUESTION: When I right-click on the taskbar and select "Show Windows Stacked" (in Vista), all the windows don't show up stacked on my Desktop. Another one is still on the taskbar but doesn't get stacked.

ANSWER: These "window" actions only work for the windows that are open on your desktop. Any windows that are minimized to the taskbar will not be included in tiling, stacking, cascading, or other window auto-arranging actions. That said, some programs, such as Filemaker Pro, will not stack, tile, or cascade even if it's open on the Desktop.

QUESTION: How can I tile some, but not all, of my windows?

ANSWER: See previous answer. If you don't want some windows to be tiled or cascaded on the screen, minimize those windows first.

QUESTION: When I mouse over the IE taskbar icon, sometimes thumbnails for all the open pages show, sometimes only one thumbnail shows, and sometimes just the title of a page shows. How can I make all thumbnails show every time?

ANSWER: On an old computer, or if your PC isn't powerful enough to show the thumbnails, only the icon for the program (the Internet Explorer "e" for example) or the title of the page may show up—not the actual thumbnail. If you have any unneeded programs open, try closing them to see if it helps your PC's performance.

Quick Launch toolbar

QUESTION: Is there a way to increase the size of the icons in the Quick Launch toolbar?

ANSWER: There are two settings for those icons: small and large. Right-click on an empty part of the Quick Launch toolbar and click on *View* to access those settings. If you can't get to an empty part of the QL toolbar, or you can't get a menu that has an option called *View*, drag the vertical divider (also known as the resizing bar) to the right to make the QL toolbar wider first, or make the taskbar taller. Then try again.

QUESTION: How do I remove items from my Quick Launch toolbar?

ANSWER: You can right-click and select Delete or drag it from the QL toolbar to your desktop and then delete it.

QUESTION: Is there any way to get my QL toolbar back in Windows 7?

ANSWER: Yes. Make sure your taskbar is not locked. I suggest you drag your taskbar to double the height before you begin. Then right-click on an empty area of the taskbar, point to Toolbars, and then click *New toolbar.* In the dialog box that opens, type in this string of text: **%AppData%\Microsoft\Internet Explorer\Quick Launch** and click *Select Folder.* The QL toolbar with the text *Quick Launch* will appear on the taskbar on the right. Drag the QL toolbar to the left side of the taskbar (just to the right of the Start Button). Right-click on it and clear *Show Text* and *Show Title* if you only want to see icons.

If you want to change the size of the icons, right-click on the QL toolbar, point to View and select large or small icons.

System Tray/Notification Area

QUESTION: There are a bunch of items on my System Tray that I don't care about. How can I hide them?

ANSWER: Right-click on the taskbar and click on Properties. The Taskbar and Start menu Properties menu should open with the taskbar menu showing on top. In Windows 7 there will be a Customize button where you can decide if you want Windows to always hide, always show, or show a program icon only when there is a notification.

In XP there should be an option called "Hide Inactive Icons" that you can check. You can also hide the clock if you want. An arrow pointing up will show on the left of the tray. Click on that if you ever want to see those hidden icons. If you have Vista, you will get an annoying message at least a couple of times in the future that says "Some of your icons are hidden. Click here to view them." Click on the X to close the message and hope that it eventually goes away for good.

QUESTION: My clock doesn't tell the right time.

ANSWER: Click on the time (double-click with XP) and click on *Change/Adjust Date and Time*. If you're connected to the Internet (this doesn't work with dial-up connections), you can have your clock synchronize with the Internet. Or you can adjust the time yourself. Make sure you click on the time zone tab and select the correct time zone. Click the *Daylight Savings* checkbox if applicable.

QUESTION: Can I show the date along with the time on the taskbar?

ANSWER: The date will show up if your taskbar is tall enough. If it's not tall enough, drag the top horizontal edge of the taskbar up. With Vista you can click on the Sidebar icon to make the Clock show on your desktop and customize it so that the calendar and clock both show.

QUESTION: I tried to drag the Internet Explorer icon down to the right of the clock but when I let go of the mouse, the IE icon doesn't show up there.

ANSWER: You can only move an item on the taskbar to another location within that taskbar *area*. This means you can move the Quick Launch toolbar items around on the QL toolbar; the programs or open windows around on the programs area (the middle part) of the taskbar; and the notification items around on the notification area. You can't move something from one area to another. You can, however, *copy* a program from the QL toolbar to the programs area.

QUESTION: I know I'm not supposed to just remove my flash drive, but I don't have one of those icons that I can click for permission.

ANSWER: The icon for removing media may be hidden. Click on the arrow (triangle pointing up) to the left of the notification area to see hidden icons. You can have the icon always show or show only for notifications by selecting *Customize* and making changes. If you can't find that arrow, open My Computer and right-click on the flash drive to eject it. (It won't actually eject. You have to remove it.)

Desktop

QUESTION: My desktop icons have disappeared—every single one. How do I get them back?

ANSWER: Right-click on your desktop and highlight *Arrange Icons By* (XP) or *View* (Vista and Windows 7). In the drop-down menu that appears, *Show Desktop Icons* probably won't have a checkmark next to it because hopefully, it somehow got turned off. So click on *Show Desktop* Icons. It takes several seconds for Windows to reset the Desktop. If that option is already checked, try unchecking it, click OK and exit, then go back in and click on *Show Destop* again to reset it..

If resetting doesn't work, then right-click on the desktop, highlight *Arrange/Sort Icons By* and click on *Name* to see if they show up again. If that doesn't work, restart your computer. If that doesn't work, you may have to do a System Restore to go back to a previous day when everything was working normally.

QUESTION: I can't move the icons on my desktop.

ANSWER: Right-click on your desktop. Point to *Arrange Icons By* (XP) or *View* (Windows 7) and look at the menu items that pop up. *Align to Grid* or *Auto Arrange* is probably checked. Click to uncheck it. If a particular arrangement is checked (arrange by name, arrange by type, etc.) uncheck that as well.

QUESTION: Everything on my desktop is suddenly huge—the icons, the folders, the words—and I can't see everything without scrolling.

ANSWER: Your screen resolution has somehow switched to a low resolution, perhaps 800 x 600. Follow the instructions in Chapter 6 in the section "Customizing Your Desktop" to change the resolution to a higher setting, which will make the items smaller.

QUESTION: I chose a higher resolution for my desktop because everything looked so big. Now it looks smaller but everything is tall and skinny. How can I get items to look proportional?

ANSWER: When selecting a resolution, it's best to choose a ratio that matches your screen size. For instance, if the width of your screen measures 16 inches and the height measures 12 inches, you'll want to select a resolution ratio of 4:3, such as 1600 x 1200, 1152 x 864, 1024 x 768, or 800 x 600. All of these choices match the 4:3 ratio. You *can* choose a different ratio setting, but items may be slightly distorted or there may be a black band either horizontally or vertically where the screen isn't being used. My Windows 7 PC only allows me to select the correct ratios for resolution. My Windows XP laptop lets me select any resolution setting I want, and I live with the consequences.

QUESTION: I changed the background on my Windows 7 desktop, and instead of saving it to my customized theme, Windows saved it as a new unsaved theme. How can I save this new background to the theme I already named?

ANSWER: Currently, there is no way to do that, but all you need do is delete your old theme and save your new theme with the same name. You delete the old one so you don't have two themes named the same. It won't bother Windows if you have two themes named the same, but it may be confusing for you.

QUESTION: I have Windows 7 but when I mouse over the Show Desktop area on my taskbar, the Preview Desktop feature doesn't work.

ANSWER: First, this feature only works with Aero themes so make sure that's what you've chosen. Then check your taskbar properties to make sure that "Use Aero Peek to Preview the Desktop" is checked.

Minimize, Maximize, Restore, Close

QUESTION: I maximized my window and then tried to drag in the corner to make the window smaller, but my pointer won't turn into a two-headed arrow.

ANSWER: Maximize means full screen. You can't resize a window in Maximized view. Click on the Restore button and then resize the window.

QUESTION: When I click the Restore button, my window doesn't move or change sizes, and it still fills the screen.

ANSWER: While in the Restored view, you probably resized the window manually to fill the screen—instead of clicking on the Maximize button. To fix it, click the Restore button and resize the window back to the size and location you want. Now every time you click Restore, the window will be restored to this new size and location—even if you close the window and open it again.

Folders

QUESTION: In XP I was able to see and copy the full path of a folder in the Address bar with back slashes between folders, but in Windows 7 I can't. Is there a way to change that back?

ANSWER: No, but you can work around it. In Windows 7, to see the full address displayed that way, click anywhere to the right of the path in the address bar or right-click any part of the address bar and choose Edit Address. The right-click shortcut menu includes additional options that allow you to copy the current address to the clipboard. Click Copy Address to save the location in a format that's optimized for copying and pasting folders in Windows Explorer, or use Copy Address As Text if you plan to paste the folder path into a document. To copy the full path for an individual file, hold down the Shift key as you right-click the file, and then choose Copy As Path. This option is especially useful if you've found a file in Windows Explorer and you want to upload it to a web site or open it in another program without browsing to the same location in an "Open" dialog box.

QUESTION: As a rule, I like my folders to open in the same window so I don't have a bunch of open folders on my desktop, but occasionally I want two folders to open in separate windows. Is there a way to open a folder in a separate window without changing that default setting?

ANSWER: That setting only applies if you open a window from within a window. If you go back to a different folder, you can open two at one time. For example, if you have a shortcut to My Documents, and you open that folder, it will show up in a window. If you go back to that shortcut and open My Documents again, it will show up in a second window. Another way to do this is to press the Shift key and double-click on the folder to open it in a separate window, OR right-click on the folder you want to open into a separate window and choose *Open in new window.*

Files

QUESTION: Sometimes when I click to select an icon, the cursor blinks in the name, and I can't move the icon.

ANSWER: Just hit your Esc key if you didn't mean to click in the name, and select it again.

QUESTION: When I try to rename an icon, a message warns me that if I change it, the file will be unreadable.

ANSWER: This happens if the icon had a file extension showing and you deleted the extension when you changed the name. When you get that message, you have the choice of continuing or canceling. Cancel and try again. This time, leave the extension alone and just rename the file name part.

QUESTION: Someone sent me a tif image file but it wouldn't display on my website. I was told it needed to be a jpg or png or gif file to display correctly, so I tried changing the extension to each of those. Still no luck. What do I do?

ANSWER: You can't just change a file type by renaming the file because different file types have different properties. To change a tif file to a jpg file, open the tif file in some type of image program

(Windows Paint will do) and then choose *File > Save as >* and select jpg as the type of file to save it to. The image program will ensure that the needed properties are saved with the new file. Note, though, that not every file can be changed to another type of file. You can tell what a file can be changed to by the choices you're given in the *Save As* dialog box.

QUESTION: I know I can open recent items from the Start menu, but is there a way to see recent items within a program, say Microsoft Word?

ANSWER: Yes. Most programs have a "Recent" file list. Inside the program, click on each item on your menu bar for the word "Preferences" or "Options" and see if you can add the option for showing recent files. In Microsoft Word, for example, click on *File > Options > Advanced* and scroll down to the Display section where you're given a choice as to how many recent documents you want MS Word to list. The more items listed, the more likely you'll find the file you're looking for. As with all other *Recent* options, files are kept track of only after the option is set.

Internet

QUESTION: On a couple of the machines I use, I find myself continually turning on the status bar in IE (*View > Status Bar*). Why doesn't IE keep this setting after I set it?

ANSWER: IE takes the last instance's settings as the default, so if you have window A showing a status bar and window B without one, whichever widow you close last sets the default for the next time IE opens. So if you want a setting to stick, make sure you only have one window open, set it the way you want, then close it. IE and Windows Explorer may share this setting; if you want the Status bar to show in all IE windows, you may need to open a folder in Windows Explorer, show the Status bar, then apply that view to all folders.

QUESTION: I want to customize my Command bar, but when I right-click, "Customize" isn't one of my choices.

ANSWER: Don't give up. The Command bar is tricky because there may not be a blank spot to click on, but I find I'm more likely to get the correct pop-up menu if I click just below the Command bar icons than if I click above them. OR if the Command bar is on a line with another bar (such as Favorites), you can drag the divider line toward the Favorites temporarily, which will expand the Command bar to its width limits. Then you can click at the beginning or end of the bar.

QUESTION: In earlier versions of IE, I could always tell what URL I was at, but since the last update, I can't because that Address bar window is not wide enough.

ANSWER: Right-click on an empty area of the IE tab area and choose "Show tabs on a separate row." Once the tabs are showing below the Address bar, there should be room to see the URL in the Address bar. You may need to enlarge your window, depending on how long the URL is.

You've reached the end of *BASICS Of Windows The Easy Guide to Your PC*. I hope this book has helped you to better use your computer. Please consider posting a review at your retailer's website.

If there are other Windows-based softwares you're interested in learning, please contact me through my website, *StephieSmith.com*.

Thanks for reading, and happy computing!

The End

About the Author

Photo by Stephen Wee

Stephie Smith was born in Parkersburg, West Virginia, the fifth of six girls. Early years were spent making mischief and, in general, driving her parents crazy while the family migrated between Ohio, West Virginia, and Florida. In fact, her family moved so often—18 times before Stephie finished sixth grade—that some people suspected they were running from the law.

Stephie left home at 14, finished high school at 16, and enlisted in the Air Force at 18, graduating with honors from the USAF Schools of Electronics and Instrumentation. After attending several colleges and universities around the country (switching majors from Chemistry to Art to English to Psychology but never figuring out what she wanted to be when she grew up), she followed her sisters to east central Florida and settled there. She remains there today writing historical romance, humorous women's fiction, and computer how-to books. You can contact her through her website StephieSmith.com. She loves to hear from readers.

Printed in Great Britain
by Amazon

34173990R00096